MY KITCHEN

REAL FOOD FROM NEAR AND FAR

Stevie Parle

Illustrations by Ros Shiers

LYONS PRESS
Guilford, Connecticut
An imprint of Globe Pequot Press

CONTENTS

"For Rose who left too soon.
For my son not yet arrived.
And for my beautiful wife
who is always there."

This book is full of Real Food. I'm talking about proper recipes, with a voice and a point of view... things I have eaten, found, or been taught to cook, both near and far from home. This is what interests me—simple recipes that have evolved out of love, excess, necessity, or poverty. This is what I collect— the dishes of stalls and temples, homes, and cafes from around the world. The truly delicious things are not always those that cost a lot, but those that have been passed from generation to generation; you can taste their integrity. The recipes collected here have nothing to do with the menus dreamed up in basement kitchens by sleep- and light-deprived chefs. They are made by and cooked for real people.

It's good to adapt recipes, to make them appropriate for the produce, season, and equipment you have. You must be careful, though, to keep the identity of a dish intact. For example, don't reach for something to put in your dhal that would never be found in an Indian kitchen. People understand this about European food. You simply have to refine the idea: use Japanese shoyu, instead of Chinese soy sauce, in Japanese dishes; use basmati rice for north Indian cooking and a shorter grain for south Indian dishes. This is not to say you shouldn't be creative. Of course you should. However, for me, remembering the bigger picture, the context of a dish, sets boundaries that allow me to be—in many ways—

more creative. At the moment at the Dock Kitchen I have a second-hand stove and an old steakhouse grill. I try to keep the food reasonably priced and manage to cook feasts for 50, on my own, three times a week. I have had to come up with new ways to do things. Working with whatever produce and equipment you have puts constraints on what you can do, and leads to new ways of thinking about a dish or approaching a problem.

Among the recipes in this book, you may find ingredients you haven't come across before. They may require a visit to a specialist market. But that's because they are from cultures whose cooking may just be emerging where you live: you will be at the front of the line. Truly good cooks try to educate themselves about food all the time. And a trip to a new part of town to rummage in an ethnic market can be as inspiring as a vacation. I find out more every day. Some of what I have learned already I have included within each chapter. I hope it's helpful.

However, when you're in a mood less inclined to inquiry and exploration and just in need of some comfort, there are plenty of recipes here to soothe and console, from asparagus with a sauce mimosa to an almond and jam tart.

In this book you will find my favorites among the dishes I have found at home and around the world, arranged as a year of cooking in my kitchen.

January is a month for staying at home—an opportunity to slow-cook, sit by the fire, read, and generally avoid going outside. But the bleak weather doesn't necessarily mean your meals have to be bland. Delicious citrus fruits (see page 18) are here, both to save us from miserable colds and to add zest to the roots and leafy vegetables in the garden plot.

This is usually a time of year for trying to make do with what you have in store, often because you can't face going out to gather ingredients. So there are lots of recipes in this chapter that will be easy to put together. Some only require you to have a few Brussels sprouts, some pasta, and a wedge of good cheese in the kitchen. Others can give you a spicy supper from your pantry supplies.

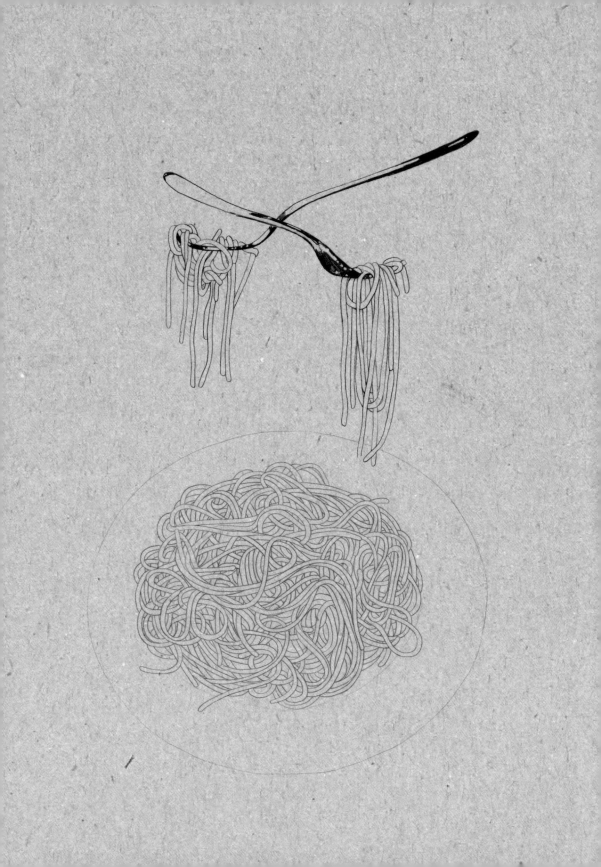

CUCINA POVERA. CHEAP SUPPERS FOR HARD TIMES IN THE NEW YEAR

THE *New Year brings cold days and hard nights, so here are warming recipes to comfort and revive. A lot of the recipes in this book, and indeed many I've found and loved around the world, are cheap to make. The best food is that which is cooked with love and attention, rather than expensive ingredients.*

CHAPATIS

THIS IS TRADITIONALLY MADE WITH WHOLE WHEAT CHAPATI FLOUR. *You can usually find this fine-grained flour in Indian markets. If you have no luck, you can substitute regular whole wheat flour, sifted, which I have used pretty successfully.*

MAKES 6
chapati flour, plus more for dusting, *4 cups*
flavorless oil, *a few tablespoons*

Put most of the flour on a work surface. Add some salt, a little oil, and enough water to make a loose, almost sticky dough. Knead until soft and silky, 2–3 minutes, adding more flour or water if needed. Form the dough into little golfballs, wrap in plastic wrap, and let rest for about 30 minutes. Then roll out each ball on a well-floured surface into a thin 7-inch round.

Place a couple of dry frying pans over high heat. Throw a chapati into each pan and cook until the base of the chapati looks dry and not doughy. Flick them straight onto the gas burner to cook for a few seconds. They will puff up. If you don't have a gas stove, flip the chapatis over and cook the other side in the pan.

CHANA MASALA

THIS IS MY FAVORITE VERSION OF THE FAMOUS CHICKPEA CURRY.
I ate it in Manali, high in the Himalayas. Use a generous bunch of cilantro.

SERVES 4
cilantro, *1 bunch*
vegetable oil, *a good slug*
cumin seeds, *1 teaspoon*
ground turmeric, *¼ teaspoon*
ground coriander, *1½ teaspoons*
Kashmiri or other mild red chile powder, *1½ teaspoons*
red onion, chopped, *1*
garlic cloves, green sprout removed, minced, *4*
fresh ginger, minced, *1-inch piece*
whole tomatoes, drained and chopped, *14-ounce can*
chickpeas, *14-ounce can*
lime wedges, *for serving*

Wash the cilantro well and separate the stems and leaves. Mince the stems. Put a wide, heavy pan over high heat and pour in the oil. When it is hot (but not smoking) add the cumin seeds. When they crackle add the other spices. Before they burn (you must move fast), add the onion, garlic, ginger, and cilantro stems. Season well. Reduce the heat, cover the pan, and let cook gently, stirring occasionally, until the flavor becomes soft and sweet, about 20 minutes.

Add the tomatoes and cook on medium heat until they have broken down, then add the chickpeas. Stir and cook together for a little while. When you are ready to eat—after you've made some chapatis (see left)—add the chopped cilantro leaves and a squeeze of lime.

HARIRA

THE TASTE OF MOROCCAN FOOD STALLS ALL OVER THE WORLD, *from the Place Djeema el-Fna in Marrakesh to the bottom of the Portobello Road in London. Harira varies from an aromatic, exotic thick soup to a watery concoction that could have come from a can. Strangely, the latter is most authentic, though here I give the former. You could add a little pasta or stir in an egg—neither addition would upset Grandma Fatima. The lamb is important for the flavor and a nice bonus for whoever gets it. If poverty decrees you must leave it out, add a little more of the onions and lentils.*

SERVES 4
olive oil
red onions, chopped, *2*
garlic cloves, green sprout removed, minced, *4*
celery with leaves, ribs and leaves chopped separately, *1 bunch*
cilantro, leaves and stems chopped separately, *1 bunch*
lamb shoulder chop, bone-in, *4 ounces*
ground black pepper, *1 heaping teaspoon*
ground ginger, *1 teaspoon*
ground coriander, *1 teaspoon*
ground cumin, *½ teaspoon*
ground turmeric, *a knifetip*
big, ripe tomato, torn into pieces, *1*
cooked brown lentils or white beans, or a mixture, *3 cups*
lemon juice, *a squeeze*
flat-leaf parsley, chopped, *½ bunch*

Pour a generous film of oil into a pan and place over low heat. Tip in the onions, garlic, celery ribs, and cilantro stems, cover, and fry very gently until soft, about 20 minutes. Add the lamb and stir until it is well coated in everything else. Season enthusiastically with salt. Add the spices and tomato and fry, increasing the heat a little, until very aromatic. Add the lentils, lemon juice, a little more oil, and a bit of water. Stir, then cover and simmer gently until the lamb is cooked, about 35 minutes. Uncover and throw in a fistful of cilantro leaves, parsley, and celery leaves.

It should be thick, earthy, and spicy. Serve with more oil on top.

DELICIOUS NOBLE ROASTED SARDINES

FROM CANNERY ROW TO COCHIN, AND FROM LISBON TO LONDON, *sardines have long been loved. I, too, adore them. When buying them fresh, they must look really beautiful: a glossy, firm-fleshed, bright red-gilled, sparkly eyed creature. There are lots of ways to cook a sardine, from grilling (the simplest and perhaps the best method) to in a curry. Or don't bother cooking them at all and have them as iwashi sushi, one of my favorites. The recipe here is the put-in-the-oven-with-some-nice-flavors style. In the summer I often tear in some tomatoes, while a few raisins, olives, and pine nuts add a Sicilian flavor. It doesn't really matter how much of each ingredient you throw in. Just add whatever you think will make your fish taste nice.*

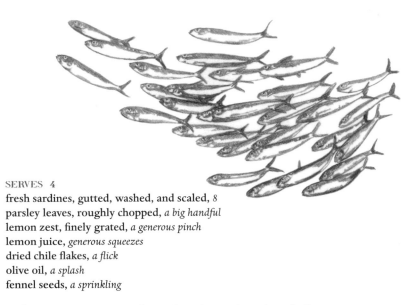

SERVES 4

fresh sardines, gutted, washed, and scaled, *8*
parsley leaves, roughly chopped, *a big handful*
lemon zest, finely grated, *a generous pinch*
lemon juice, *generous squeezes*
dried chile flakes, *a flick*
olive oil, *a splash*
fennel seeds, *a sprinkling*

Preheat the oven to 475°F. Lay the sardines in one layer in a shallow baking pan and season them well with all the other ingredients. Roast them for 2–10 minutes, depending on the size of the sardines—they're ready when the skin crinkles and the flesh can be pulled from the spine reasonably easily.

HOW TO SLOW-COOK

The key is in the name... It is very important to slow-cook slowly. You are aiming for soft, slightly gelatinous meat that falls gently from the bone. If it cooks too fast, the meat will become soft but also turn stringy and dry.

Traditionally, slow-cooking is the way both to beautify tougher cuts of meat and to use the residual heat of a bread oven after the day's baking. Sometimes I leave a pot on top of the wood-burning stove at home, to slow-cook overnight. The result is always good and I love the feeling of letting food cook itself. If you're going to abandon your dish, it's important that it shouldn't run out of liquid. Often I seal the edge of the pot with flour and water paste, which prevents much of the evaporation.

The cuts of meat that generally slow-cook best are the fattier bits that worked hardest during the life of the animal. Shanks and shoulders, ribs and necks all slow-cook well.

Often I start a slow-cooked dish by browning the meat; whether osso bucco or curry goat, it can lend a depth of flavor. Always brown well-seasoned meat in a hot pan (but not so hot that it singes), leaving a bit of space around each piece—overcrowding a pan will mean the meat boils instead of frying and it will probably end up a bit tough.

I'm not much of a stewmaker. I prefer to slow-roast cuts of meat on the bone, not chopped up into bits. The bones provide lots of flavor and the meat seems to stay more moist, too.

NEW YEAR'S DAY: A WHOLE BEEF SHANK

THIS *takes 12 hours to cook. It is a classic from Tuscany, called* peposo. *I love to have it with baked potatoes into which I have stuffed a little of the melting bone marrow. It is good to cook this on a day when you are mostly in the kitchen, drinking coffee and nursing heavy heads. The warmth from the oven and the aroma of the beef is restorative in itself. You can also cook this on the stovetop, or in the embers of a fire, as long as it goes slowly. If you get it ready, you can put it in the oven before you go to bed. Make sure the butcher cuts the narrow end from the shank, so you can get at the marrow if you want.*

SERVES 10
whole beef shank, *1*
bottles of Chianti, *4*
bulbs of garlic, unpeeled, *2*
black peppercorns, *a big handful*
coarse salt, *a big handful*
all-purpose flour, *for making a paste*

Preheat the oven to 225°F. Put all the ingredients except the flour in a Dutch oven or casserole. If the wine doesn't cover the beef, add a bit of water. Put on the lid and seal it well with some flour mixed to a paste with water. Cook in the oven for 12 hours.

Eat with baked potatoes, polenta, mashed potatoes, chard, or anything else suitably comforting.

STEAMED GINGER PUDDING

A GENEROUS AMOUNT OF GINGER GIVES THIS PUDDING A KICK.
It will help you to banish the remnants of any hangover.

SERVES 6
salted butter, *1 cup (2 sticks)*
sugar, *1 cup*
eggs, *4*
self-rising flour, sifted, *1¾ cups*
ground ginger, *3 tablespoons*
golden syrup or light corn syrup, *⅔ cup*

In an electric mixer, cream the butter and sugar together really well until white and whipped looking. Add the eggs one by one, still mixing, then add a handful of the flour with 1 tablespoon ginger to stop the eggs curdling. Fold in the remaining flour. In a 2-quart pudding basin or steamed-pudding mold, mix the rest of the ginger with the golden syrup and 2 tablespoons boiling water. Pour the batter into the mold. Cover with a piece of wax paper tied on with string, or the lid.

Steam the pudding for 2 hours. Unmold to serve hot.

CITRUS

In January, citrus fruits are very good and so welcome. Jaffa, Cara Cara, navel, blood, and Seville oranges, Meyer lemons, kaffir limes… They are available just when you need them most. Miserable weather, persistent colds, and a general lack of vibrancy are made up for, at least in part, by these beautiful, glowing orange, yellow, and green fruits.

Citrus fruits are indispensable in the kitchen, particularly lemons. A squeeze of lemon on a steak or grilled sardine can lift it beautifully, making it fresh and zingy. I often finish an Arab bean or chickpea soup with a bit of lemon as well as a slug of oil (see page 12), while my most frequently used salad dressing is simply a squeeze of lemon with salt and olive oil.

Most people won't bother to grow their own citrus fruits. The exception is the kaffir lime, which can be grown in a pot. One of my favorite plants, it has the most fantastically flavored leaves plus perfumed fruit zest and juice, which are used in all sorts of Thai dishes.

BLOOD ORANGE SALAD

BLOOD ORANGES ARE AN ESPECIALLY BEAUTIFUL CITRUS FRUIT.
This salad is often served during winter in the south of Italy.

SERVES 4
blood oranges, *2*
fennel bulbs, *2*
large salted anchovy fillets, *4*
small, hard black olives, pitted, *10*
olive oil, *for dressing*
lemon juice, *for dressing*

Cut the peel and pith carefully from the oranges. Slice the fruit into
wheels, removing the seeds as you go. Cut the tops from the fennel
bulbs, reserving any fronds, then halve them vertically. Remove the
tougher outer layer and slice across thinly into half-moons.

Halve the anchovies lengthwise. Mix everything with oil, plus lemon
if the oranges are more sweet than sour. Season with pepper.

PRESERVED LEMONS

THESE TURN OUT JUST LIKE THE GREAT ONES YOU GET IN MOROCCO.
Preserve lemons when they are really good, and cheap.

lemons
cardamom pods
black peppercorns
coarse rock salt

Cut the lemons, from top to near-bottom, almost into quarters; keep
them attached at the base. Pack a few cardamom pods and a couple of
peppercorns into each fruit. Make a layer of salt in a large sterilized jar
and add a layer of lemons. Repeat until all your lemons are used up,
packing as much salt into and around them as you can, leaving no space
for air. Leave in a dark place for at least 3 months before using.

SEVILLE ORANGE TART

I AM ALWAYS LOOKING FOR MORE WAYS TO USE SEVILLE ORANGES. *Marmalade is wonderful (although I am no expert at making it). Here is a variation on a classic lemon tart.*

SERVES 6–8
Seville oranges, *5*
sugar, *1 cup*
butter, *⅔ cup (1¼ sticks)*
whole eggs, *3*
egg yolks, *4*
8-inch sweet pastry shell, baked (see page 167)

Peel 4 of the oranges, then remove and discard all the white pith from the peel with a sharp knife. Slice the peel very thinly, then chop it a little so the pieces are not too long. Juice all the oranges. Put the juice in a pan with the orange peel and sugar. Cook over low heat for 5 minutes. Add the butter, cut into bits. Whisk the whole eggs with the yolks, and preheat the broiler.

When the butter has just melted, remove from the heat and whisk in the egg mixture. Return to the heat and cook gently, stirring, until the filling mixture is slightly thicker and translucent. Do not rush this step, because the tart filling won't be cooked again later.

Quickly pour the filling into the baked pastry shell. Broil, close to the heat, until the tart has large black spots on top, 1–2 minutes. Let cool, then eat with crème fraîche.

A COLD, WET NIGHT. A QUIET SUPPER BY THE FIRE

I LOVE *to be able to put together a great meal with just the things in the cupboard, especially when it is miserable weather outside. This was made from the only things we had —a few Brussels sprouts, a bit of cheese, and some pasta.*

BRUSSELS SPROUTS ARE DELICIOUS RAW

I FIRST ATE THIS IN A GREAT NEW YORK RESTAURANT CALLED LUPA. *I texted the idea to the chef Skye Gyngell, with whom I had been working. She was, at that very moment, with the great Maggie Beer in Australia, who immediately told her I must be eating at Lupa. It is clearly a memorable dish for other people, too.*

Brussels sprouts, *a few each*
pecorino, *1 ounce or so each*
lemon juice, *an enthusiastic squeeze*
olive oil, *a generous slug*

Shave the cleaned, very fresh sprouts on a mandoline, or with a very sharp knife, into ice water. Leave them for a while; they will become crisp. Drain and dry them. Shave some crumbly pecorino and mix with the sprouts. Add salt, squeeze some lemon over, splash with some olive oil, grind some pepper over, and eat within half an hour. It's a great snack. Or try it (as they do at Lupa) as part of a mixed antipasti, or on the side of a plate of prosciutto from Parma, or salami from Tuscany.

CACIO E PEPE PASTA

PEPPER IS A VERY IMPORTANT SPICE AND IT ALWAYS HAS BEEN SO.
*It is still vital to the economies of many regions. We've traveled to a few places
where the pepper of the area is very prestigious. In Kampot, south Cambodia,
the fresh green pepper is particularly fine and the climate well suited to its
growth. It is still used in most of the dishes there. Just over the Cambodian
border, Thais prefer to use chile, a comparative newcomer introduced from
South America by Portuguese traders and colonialists.*

*In Kerala, India, they have seven varieties of black pepper that are used for
different purposes. Keralan pepper is often thought to be the best in the world.*

*This pasta dish is all about pepper and cheese—here pecorino, which is a
sheep's cheese made all over Italy with very different results. The initial process
is the same everywhere, but after this the cheeses can be aged and finished
in vastly contrasting ways. They can be oiled, washed, thrown in wine lees
(sediment), or even covered in blood or ashes, depending on the tradition of
the region. The best cheese for this dish is a pecorino Romano, reasonably aged.
In Rome, the pasta they often use is bucatini (hollow and spaghetti-like),
which is a good choice, although fusilli, penne, or spaghetti would also hold
the sauce nicely.*

> **black peppercorns**
> **pasta,** *3 ounces or so per person*
> **pecorino Romano, finely grated,** *a big handful*
> **delicious olive oil**

Grind your best black pepper coarsely in a mortar and pestle. Boil the
pasta in a lot of salty water and, when cooked but still a little chewy (*al
dente*), drain and toss well with the cheese, a lot of pepper, and a very
bold slug of good oil. Add a little cooking water to loosen the pasta if it
needs it. You have to toss it a lot to make the sauce come together. If it
is going stringy, which it sometimes does, add a little more oil and hot
water, then stir some more.

02

February is a month to start looking toward the spring. Whether planting your tomato seeds inside, or buying hothouse rhubarb, the first shoots and blossoms of the year are all around us in the kitchen and garden.

Despite these cheering signs of the season to come, at this time of year we all need a Japanese dinner (see page 32), to restore and warm us against the last of the winter chill. It's also a good time to take a moment to ponder such important matters as umami (see page 30), before life speeds up and the spring begins to race away from us.

Leeks are practically the only thing ready in the vegetable plot right now. They can add a delicious sweetness to a soffritto (see page 182), but are perhaps at their best simply grilled whole, while still young and slender (see page 36).

ANCHOVIES

When Nicky (my wife) and I lived in New York, one of our first explorations in Manhattan led us to an excellent food shop in Chelsea Market. It's a big warehouse, with crates of bottarga, jars of tomatoes, great-quality pasta, panettone, olive oil… The place is jammed full of wonderful things. We had a little cash, so Nicky bought a beautiful big can of salted anchovies. Anchovies left in the salt in which they are cured are the best type. These were big, a good thing for an anchovy in salt to be. Anchovies are now endangered and I am deeply sad that we have abused such a precious resource. There are in fact lots of anchovies in some places and very few in others. We must leave those fragile areas alone to recover their stock. We must be sure to know where the anchovies we are eating come from (the Cantabrian coast where the best reside is off limits; the fishery there has been closed for years) and, as with all fish, we must use our buying power to influence the fishermen. It is important to eat fewer anchovies, but to respect them more and be doubly sure only to eat the very fine anchovies packed in salt, not those nasty little fishy things in tiny cans of bad oil.

I love cooking with anchovies. They give a depth and type of saltiness not normally found in Western food, but more like the fish sauce of Southeast Asia. What the Japanese call umami (see page 30) gives a name to this deliciousness.

Anchovies don't make things taste fishy, as you might expect. Roasting fishes love them and a steak will be satisfied if, in his final seconds in the pan, he is joined by his old friend Anch.

1 You first have to pull off and discard the head.

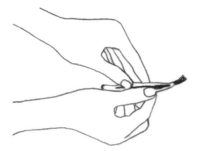

2 Then you must pull the anchovies apart under running water, easing the fillets away and discarding the bones, rinsing off some salt and rehydrating them a little in the process. I have learned never to let the anchovies sit in water; this allows the salt to penetrate the flesh too much, making it gray, and the fish salty rather than salted.

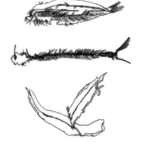

Anchovies mellow with acid. Lemon or vinegar left on an anchovy for a few minutes without oil will "cook" the anchovy slightly, giving it a quieter nature.

One of the best uses of an anchovy is on a piece of hard sourdough bread with butter. You can also toast the bread and involve a soft-cooked egg to great effect.

ANCHOVY – ALMOND PASTE

A RECIPE FROM ELIZABETH DAVID'S *FRENCH PROVINCIAL COOKING*. *Serve it on toast before you start a meal.*

SERVES 4
lemon, ½
anchovy fillets, 4
garlic clove, green sprout removed, ¼
mint leaves, 10
whole blanched almonds, 3 tablespoons
red wine vinegar, about 1 tablespoon
good, delicate olive oil, about 7 tablespoons

Squeeze a bit of lemon juice over the anchovies.

Crush the garlic in a mortar with a little coarse salt until smooth. Add the mint and continue to pestle. When broken down, add the anchovies and grind until fine. Now put in the almonds and crush them up until everything's smooth once more.

Add the bit of vinegar and continue to mix with the pestle, then very slowly pour in the olive oil, stirring all the time. Thin down with water, if necessary, until the emulsion is a little thicker than heavy cream.

A QUICK ANCHOVY SAUCE

THIS ADDS DEPTH AND DELICIOUSNESS TO ALMOST ANYTHING. *There must be an infinite variety of anchovy sauces, and they enhance practically any plain grilled fish, meat, or vegetable.*

ENOUGH FOR 4 SERVINGS OF MOST THINGS
anchovy fillets, 4
salted capers, well rinsed, 1 tablespoon
red wine vinegar, 1 tablespoon
dried, small, hot chile, crushed, 1
oregano leaves, chopped, 1 tablespoon
good olive oil, 7 tablespoons

Chop the anchovies and capers and put them in a little bowl. Pour the vinegar over them. Add the chile and oregano to the anchovy mixture. Leave for a few minutes, then slowly stir in the olive oil. Taste and add more vinegar or chile, if needed.

BAGNA CAUDA

BOTH THE METHOD AND THE INGREDIENTS ARE CONTENTIOUS...
*But this is the case with most classic recipes. Some say bagna cauda must be
served with raw vegetables and garlic, others that both must be cooked. It is
generally accepted that using a red wine such as Barolo instead of milk is
sacrilege, although I think it's delicious. In fact, I like all the variations. This
recipe is to be served with boiled vegetables. Depending on the season, use a
varied mix of cauliflower, artichokes, cardoons, carrots, asparagus, Swiss
chard stalks, beets, and squash. Blanch them in salted water (cook any strongly
flavored vegetables separately). Make sure they are all soft but not mushy, and
drain very well before you pour the sauce over them.*

SERVES 6

garlic cloves, green sprout removed, *4*
milk, *1 cup*
anchovy fillets, minced, *10*
olive oil, *2 tablespoons*
red wine vinegar, *a splash*
unsalted butter, *½ cup (1 stick)*

Cook the garlic gently with the milk in a small, heavy-based pan
until the milk has reduced to just a few tablespoons and the garlic is
completely soft. Squash the garlic cloves to a mush with a wooden
spoon, then grind in some black pepper and add the anchovies.

Continue cooking, while mushing up the bits of anchovy with the
back of your spoon, to make a melted paste.

Whisk in the olive oil and vinegar, still over the heat. Chop the butter
into cubes the size of playing dice and add them to the sauce one by
one, whisking and waiting until each piece of butter has completely
melted before adding the next.

Taste. You may need more vinegar, although
the sauce isn't supposed to be too
acidic. If it is too delicate, add a few
more crushed anchovies. If it needs
salt you probably don't have enough
anchovy in it. Keep the sauce warm in
a hot-water bath until you are ready
to eat.

UMAMI

Of the five basic tastes we can detect on our palates, umami is the least well known. Some describe it as depth or fullness of flavor. I say it is savory deliciousness. Umami is something I have known about for a long time, but not consciously. All good cooks sense it and aim for it in their food, but learning about it purposely is a kind of revelation.

Italian cooks know so much about umami that I'm surprised they've never given it a name. Italians use loads of umami-rich seasonings—such as dried mushrooms and Parmesan—in their cooking all the time.

Umami is an idea natural to the Japanese, so natural that, when buying Parmesan in the Tokyo Midtown branch of the New York deli, Dean and Deluca, I was informed by my Japanese server that the three-year-old Reggiano had more umami and less salt than the regular two-year-old.

This is why Parmesan is such a great seasoning. It doesn't make things taste of Parmesan, or salty, it just makes things taste more. Turns the volume up.

I immediately thought about my friend Gillian when I was told about Parmesan umami. Gillian is a chef, scholar, and Parmesan nut. She once told me that the way Parmesan is aged makes the sodium change to monosodium glutamate (MSG). Presumably this conversion continues the longer it is aged; therefore, there's more MSG in the three-year-aged cheese… just as the Japanese lady in the deli told me. I am convinced that a similar process happens as cured meats age; they certainly develop a deeper umami, and some, such as the very best Spanish hams, even contain crystals in their silky slices that seem similar to those in aged Parmesan.

MSG occurs naturally in quite a few foods in varying quantities. It has umami itself, but it is a little more complex than that. MSG received a bad reputation when people thought the massive quantities of the commercially produced chemical added to bad Chinese takeouts made them ill. Apparently it wasn't the chemical but the food itself. Overuse of MSG in the Chinese takeout fashion simply makes everything taste the same.

Many of the building blocks of Japanese cooking are umami-rich, such as miso, shoyu (soy), and the dried kenbo (edible kelp) and katsuobushi (dried bonito flakes) that together form the dashi (stock) used in so many dishes. It is apparently the naturally high levels of inosinic acid (a commonly-used flavor enhancer) in katsuobushi that gives it its high umami level.

There are many umami-rich flavors in Western cooking, too: Parmesan, porcini, salted anchovies, truffles, beef, and tomatoes come first to mind. Something amazing happens to a good slow-cooked soffritto—the Italian fried vegetable base (called sofrito in Spanish)—that surely gives it umami. And, perhaps, the browning of meat also increases its umami.

Once you have identified the taste of it you will find yourself more consciously using ingredients to add the umami dimension to lots of dishes you cook, and perhaps realizing how much you did so before you knew its name.

A RESTORATIVE JAPANESE SUPPER FOR THOSE IN NEED OF A LITTLE ZEN.

PROPER *Zen cooking (in common with many other religious diets, from that of the Indian Brahmans to that of Catholic monks) uses no onion or garlic, little oil, and few strong flavors. So this is not a "proper" Zen meal. It is delicious all the same, and gave us the calm and comfort we were looking for.*

You should view this meal as a progression. Start with the sea kale and then maybe make a little tempura (see page 60). Have the tofu and then a few other things at the same time: a bowl of Japanese rice, some plain white fish, spinach, and the miso with clams. You will find yourself restored.

CLAMS MISO SOUP

SERVES 4
miso paste, *3 tablespoons*
dashi, *2½ cups*
fresh littleneck clams, *1 pound*
scallion, white part only, very thinly sliced, *1*

Dissolve the miso in the dashi in a large pan, then add the clams. Cover and simmer until the clams open. Decant everything into bowls, straining the liquid through cheesecloth to remove any grit, and add a couple of slices of scallion to each serving.

SILKEN TOFU AND TINY ANCHOVIES

BEFORE I LIVED IN JAPAN, I DIDN'T REALLY APPRECIATE TOFU. *There if you walk through the streets of any residential area early in the morning, you will usually come across an old man in a wooden shop making fresh tofu. That really is a revelation. There are several types of tofu, ranging in texture from firm to soft, depending on how much liquid is drained away. Silken tofu is drained through silk; it has a softer texture because less liquid escapes. You can buy silken tofu and the dried anchovies used here from Japanese and Korean markets.*

SERVES 4
silken tofu, *1 block*
toasted sesame oil, *½ cup*
tiny dried anchovies, *4 ounces*
good-quality Japanese shoyu (soy sauce), *to season*

Cut the tofu into 1½-inch blocks and carefully put on little plates. Heat a small pan with the sesame oil. When hot, add the anchovies. Fry until crisp and light brown. Put a little pile of anchovies on top of each piece of tofu, then sprinkle a few drops of good shoyu over.

SEA KALE IN TEN-TSUYU

SEA KALE IS ONE OF THE FIRST SIGNS OF EARLY SPRING IN THE UK. *This cabbage-like vegetable is also found on the Pacific Coast, and can be grown in vegetable gardens. I've given another version of ten-tsuyu on page 62, to be served with tempura, but there are lots of types. This one is more delicate. If you are unable to buy sea kale, substitute with kale, collard greens, swiss chard, mustard greens, or spinach.*

SERVES 4
for the ten-tsuyu
dashi (soup stock), *about ⅔ cup*
mirin (sweet cooking wine), *about ¼ cup*
shoyu (soy sauce), *about ¼ cup*

for the sea kale
sea kale, *1 bunch*

Make the ten-tsuyu by warming the dashi, then seasoning with the mirin and shoyu. Taste and balance the mixture carefully.

Briefly boil the sea kale in salted water until soft, then chop it into 1½-inch pieces. Make a little pile of sea kale in a small dish and pour the warm sauce over it.

LEEKS

At this time of year, the vegetable garden is pretty bare. There may be some rhubarb doing its best to poke up through the cold soil, but there's not much else apart from the stalwart leeks standing in the frost like stiff, green soldiers. An allium such as garlic and onions, it is not quite as strong and is an excellent choice when you need a subtle, sweet onion flavor. Make sure to wash leeks well: those layers can harbor grit and soil.

LEEKS WITH SAUCE GRIBICHE

SERVES 4

for the sauce gribiche
small red onion, minced, ¼
capers, rinsed and chopped, *a few*
anchovy fillets, chopped, *2*
cornichons (gerkins), chopped, *a few*
wine vinegar, *about 1 tablespoon*
parsley, leaves only, minced, *½ bunch*
tarragon, leaves only, minced, *½ bunch*
chervil, leaves only, minced, *½ bunch*
Dijon mustard, *1 teaspoon*
eggs, hard-cooked (see page 59), *4*
olive oil, *about ⅔ cup*

for the leeks
small leeks, trimmed and washed, *1 or 2 per person*

Put the onion, capers, anchovies, and cornichons in a bowl. Pour in the vinegar and stir, then leave to allow the onion to mellow. Mix in the herbs. Add the mustard and lots of black pepper. Peel the eggs, then break them up in the sauce. Boil the leeks in salty water until tender, about 5 minutes. Drain very well. Gradually stir the oil into the sauce, then check for salt and acidity. Eat with the warm boiled leeks.

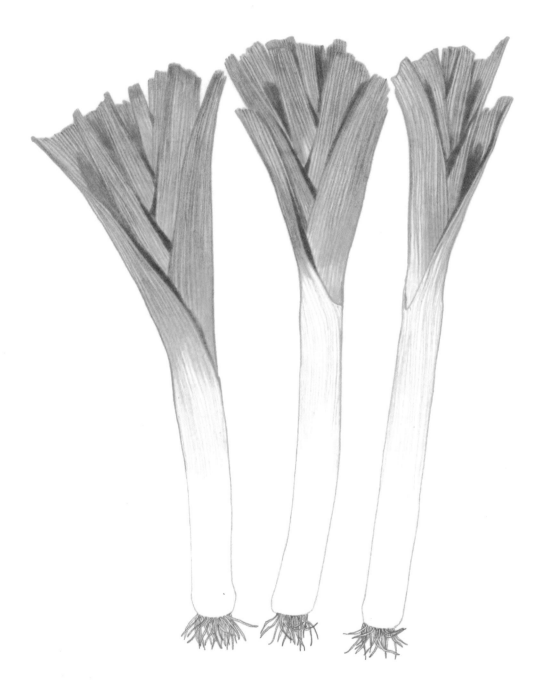

GRILLED LEEKS WITH ROMESCO SAUCE

A CLASSIC CATALAN DISH MADE IN LATE WINTER OR EARLY SPRING. *There, instead of leeks, they often use calcots, the first sweet white onions of the year, and they grill them over charcoal. Although you can get away with using a food processor and stirring, the sauce won't be as good as it is when made by crushing and pounding. So if you don't have a large mortar and pestle, I recommend that you buy one. Agridulce paprika may be hard to find unless you have a Spanish market nearby (if you can't find it, just use more of the other two paprikas, to taste). Look for Valencia or Marcona almonds there, too.*

ENOUGH FOR 10 PEOPLE
whole plum tomatoes from a can, drained and rinsed, 4
whole almonds, *1 cup*
garlic cloves, *6*
olive oil, *1 cup*
coarse, dry bread crumbs, *¾ cup*
Albarino wine, *a small glass*
hot paprika, *to taste*
paprika agridulce, *to taste*
sweet paprika, *to taste*
sherry vinegar, *2 tablespoons*

Preheat the oven to 350°F. Roast the tomatoes for 25 minutes. Roast the almonds until starting to brown, 5–10 minutes. Gently fry 5 of the garlic cloves, unpeeled, in half the olive oil in a small saucepan. When the garlic is a deep brown, but not burned, remove it and discard. Fry the bread crumbs in the flavored oil over medium heat until they are crisp and deep brown. As soon as they are ready, drain in a strainer and spread out on paper towels.

Peel the remaining garlic clove (remove the green sprout if there is one), then crush it in a large mortar and pestle. Add the almonds and pound until you have a thick, coarse paste. To the little glass of wine add a scant teaspoon of hot paprika, the same of agridulce, and a little more of the sweet paprika. Stir with the wine, then add to the almonds. Add the tomatoes and continue to pound. When reasonably amalgamated, stir in the remaining oil and the vinegar. Add the crumbs a few minutes before you eat. Taste and adjust the balance.

To grill young leeks: Remove the outer layer, slit the leek two-thirds of the way down, and wash well inside (they are always gritty). Grill over a cool area of the coals until soft and tender. Peel off any burned layers. Two leeks each is about right if they are small.

LEEK, POTATO, AND PORCINI SOUP

THIS IS A PERFECT RECIPE TO MAKE FROM THE KITCHEN PANTRY.
That doesn't mean it is dull though. The dried porcini lend a deep umami flavor to the soup, and the leeks a little sweetness, while the potatoes add the heft and comfort we all need during February.

SERVES 4
dried porcini, *2 ounces*
large leeks, *4*
waxy potatoes (or new, round white, or round red potatoes), *7 ounces*
carrot, *1*
red onion, *1*
celery heart, *1*
olive oil, *a splash*
dried, small, hot chile, crushed, *1*
garlic cloves, green shoot removed, coarsely chopped, *2*
whole plum tomatoes from a can, drained and rinsed, *3*
parsley, coarsely chopped, *a small handful*

Soak the porcini in 1 cup boiling water. Slice the leeks. Peel the potatoes and boil them in well-salted water until tender; drain. Coarsely chop the carrot, onion, and celery, then start them frying in olive oil. Season with the chile, salt, and lots of pepper. After a few minutes, add the garlic. Cover and cook, stirring occasionally, until very soft and sweet, 15–20 minutes. Drain the porcini, reserving the soaking liquid.

Add the tomatoes and porcini to the carrot and onion. Break up the tomato with the back of a wooden spoon, then add the sliced leeks and parsley. Cook gently until the leeks are soft. Add the potatoes. Let the potatoes absorb the flavor, breaking them up a bit with your spoon. Add the porcini soaking liquid and enough water to make a thick soup. Finish with a splash of olive oil and check the seasoning.

03

In many places the soil has not yet woken up, and vegetable gardens are still bare, but March brings spring produce from other warmer climates. Try some of my artichoke recipes (see page 42) to take advantage of this good fortune.

I often like to turn my hand to more exotic food at this time of year. The Sri Lankan feast here (see page 46) will bring the taste of sunshine as well as welcome memories or daydreams of far away places. Getting the Spice Right (see page 50) will help you import an exotic flavor into your own March kitchen.

This is a good time of year for baking, to be enveloped in the sweet fragrance and warmth of a kitchen while it's still chilly outside. My torta della nonna (see page 53) should bring you this comfort.

ARTICHOKES

At this time of year, delicious globe artichokes come into their peak season. They vary in size from baby artichokes, which can be eaten whole, to the familiar medium-sized or large globes. Occasionally you will see violet and other special artichokes. When buying, the most important thing is to be sure they are fresh and beautiful, with tightly closed leaves. An artichoke is the bud of a (very beautiful) flower; the longer they grow, the tougher and more "chokey" they become.

HOW TO PREPARE AN ARTICHOKE

The standard way of boiling artichokes whole and eating them with melted butter is nice, but limiting. In other cuisines the preparations are more varied.

1. First choose a good artichoke that feels as if the leaves are in a nice tight cluster (more a bud than a flower).

2. Tear off the leaves one by one, starting from the base. Do not snap them off, or you'll risk losing some of the precious heart.

3. As you work, you will notice the color of the leaves changes from dark green at the base to paler, softer green toward the tip. When you reach leaves that are about half this light green shade, stop peeling.

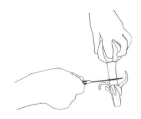

4. Peel the stalk, and then the dark green part from the outside of the heart.

5. Trim off the stalk, leaving about 6 inches in situ.

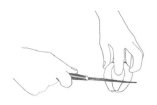

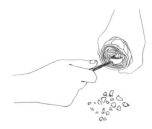

6. Cut the artichoke horizontally at the point where the color changes.

7. Scoop out any hairy choke from inside. If you've been lucky enough to find young, tender artichokes, there shouldn't be much.

8. Keep the prepared artichoke in slightly lemony water until you cook it. The lemon will prevent discoloration, to which artichokes are prone.

ARTICHOKES COOKED THE ROMAN WAY

CARCIOFI ALLA ROMANA IS AMONG THE BEST ARTICHOKE RECIPES. *I love it as a first course with cured ham. It is delicious both hot or at room temperature.*

SERVES 5 GREEDY PEOPLE,
OR 10 LESS HUNGRY SOULS
artichokes, prepared, stalks left about 4 inches long, *10*
parsley leaves, *a handful*
mint leaves, *a handful*
garlic cloves, peeled, green sprout removed, *3*
white wine, *1 glass*
olive oil, *⅓ cup*

Find a pot that will hold your artichokes snugly with their stalks in the air, so they won't topple over during cooking. Throw in the herbs and garlic. Pour in the wine and oil, then add enough water to reach just below where the heart turns into stalk. Cover with parchment paper and put on the lid. Steam on medium heat for about 20 minutes (check after 15 that the liquid hasn't all evaporated; add more if it has).

When the hearts are soft, uncover and increase the heat so the water evaporates and the artichokes begin to fry. Let them get nicely brown, then serve with the sizzled herbs and bits of leaves that have fallen off.

RAW ARTICHOKE SALAD

YOU CAN ADD PARMESAN, CAPERS, OR GRATED BOTTARGA (TUNA OR GREY MULLET EGG MASS) TO THIS.

SERVES 4
artichokes, prepared, *4*
lemon juice
parsley, chopped, *a few leaves*
good olive oil

Carefully slice the artichokes very thinly lengthwise. Put the slices in a bowl and sprinkle with lemon juice to prevent discoloration. Add the parsley. Season, squeeze more lemon over, and pour on some oil. Mix well and taste. They should be well-dressed but not swimming.

ARTICHOKE PILAF

I OFTEN MAKE A PILAF WITH JUST NUTS, OR CAULIFLOWER OR PEAS…
*whatever is in season. It's a great dish to have in your repertoire. Adjust the
seasonings according to what you fancy and eat with yogurt.*

SERVES 4
basmati rice, *2 cups*
red onions, *2*
butter, *⅔ cup (1¼ sticks)*
allspice berries, crushed, *1 tablespoon*
black cumin seeds, *1 teaspoon*
cinnamon stick, *¾-inch piece*
artichokes, prepared, *4 large or 6 small*
parsley leaves, chopped, *a handful*
dill, chopped, *a sprig or two*
mint, chopped, *a sprig or two*

Rinse the rice. Soak in warm water for at least 30 minutes, then drain.

Meanwhile, cut the onions quite finely and fry slowly in the butter
with the spices until soft and sweet, about 20 minutes, stirring
occasionally. Season well.

Halve the artichokes, then add them to the onions. Pour in ½ cup
water and cover the pot. Steam until the artichokes are soft, about
10 minutes. Increase the heat and add the rice. Stir once or twice to
coat the rice with the spicy butter, but be careful not to break the grains.

When the rice is hot, add enough hot water to cover by ¾ inch. Cover
with parchment paper and then a lid. Continue to cook on medium-
high heat for a few minutes, then reduce the heat to very low and cook
for 5 minutes longer. Remove from the heat and leave, still covered, for
about 10 minutes so the rice can finish steaming. Fluff up with a fork
and sprinkle on the herbs.

EARLY MORNING ON THE DECK WITH CIAMBELLINE, WATCHING THE CHERRY BLOSSOM ON THE BANK

CIAMBELLINE

A LOVELY RECIPE FROM A FUNNY ITALIAN BOOK: *FANTASIA D'ERBE*, *by Fausto Oneto. He calls it Nonna Tina's ring cake. It makes an excellent breakfast with a cup of coffee and it will last for a few days. But it's also delicious with a glass of sweet wine.*

SERVES 4

all-purpose flour, sifted, plus more for the pan, *1¾ cups*
sugar, *1 cup*
baking powder, *1 teaspoon*
salt, *a pinch*
egg yolk, *1*
ricotta cheese, *1¼ cups*
orange, finely grated zest and juice, *1*
vanilla extract, *a few drops*
butter, *for the pan*

Preheat the oven to 350°F.

Mix the flour, sugar, baking powder, and salt in a bowl. Make a well in the center and add the egg yolk, ricotta, orange zest, and vanilla. Mix well, adding enough orange juice to make a soft dough. Knead it a little, then roll the dough into a sausage and coil it into a buttered and floured 10-inch tube pan.

Bake until a skewer inserted into the cake comes out clean, about 40 minutes. Let cool in the pan.

A SRI LANKAN SUPPER TO BRING NEW RECIPES AND A BIT OF SUNSHINE TO OLD FRIENDS.

I SPENT *a few months on a beautiful tea plantation called Samakanda in the south of Sri Lanka. Samakanda means "peaceful hill," and it is a beautiful place. I would spend the morning helping on the plantation, then return to cabins at the top of the hill to watch Anoka, the cook, create amazing dishes from the shoots and leaves growing wild and domestic throughout Samakanda. The plantation was set up by Rory Spowers, who bought it as a ruin, rediscovering it and bringing it slowly back to life. Back in London, it was a real pleasure to get together with my friends Rose Gray and David Macllwaine, fellow Ceylon enthusiasts, and spend a day cooking the country's wonderful food. I was especially delighted to find some of the near-mythical green gotu kola for sale in a Sri Lankan market, which made the feast even more authentic. All this food is so delicious and exotic that it makes you feel as if you are on vacation. I love sharing the recipes I have found in my travels.*

COCONUT BROTH
WITH POTATO OR SQUASH

THIS TYPICALLY SRI LANKAN DISH IS VERY QUICK AND EASY TO MAKE.
*Maldive fish is the Sri Lankan equivalent to fish sauce, although it is dry. If
you cannot find it, you can substitute a rinsed, salted anchovy fillet.*

SERVES 6 AS PART OF A BIG SELECTION
waxy potatoes or sweet squash, in ¾-inch dice, *8 ounces (about 2 cups)*
red onion, minced, *1*
fresh, hot green chile, left whole, *1 or 2*
fresh curry leaves, *a small handful*
garlic clove, green shoot removed, chipped, *1*
fresh ginger, minced, *½-inch piece*
ground turmeric, *a knifetip*
fenugreek seeds, *25 or so*
black pepper, freshly ground, *½ teaspoon*
Maldive fish, *1 teaspoon*
coconut milk, *2 cups*
lime juice, *to taste*

> **RED RICE** I buy round-grain
> Sri Lankan or Keralan rice whenever
> I see it. Rinse it well, then cook as
> you would any other rice.

Put everything except the coconut milk and lime in a pan. Pour in 1 cup
water. Bring to a boil, then reduce the heat, cover, and cook until the
potatoes or squash are soft, about 10 minutes. Add the coconut milk,
and lime juice and salt to taste.

CASHEW NUT CURRY

ONE OF THE BEST AND SIMPLEST SRI LANKAN DISHES I HAVE FOUND.

SERVES 6 AS PART OF A BIG SELECTION
raw cashew nuts, *2 heaping cups*
coconut milk, *1¼ cups*
ground turmeric, *½ teaspoon*
hot chile powder, *¼ teaspoon*
cinnamon stick, *¾-inch piece*
Maldive fish, *½ teaspoon*
anise seed, *¼ teaspoon*
sunflower oil, *1 tablespoon*
fresh curry leaves, *20*

Put all the ingredients except the oil and curry leaves in a saucepan and
simmer for about 10 minutes, then season with salt. Pour the oil into a
frying pan and, when hot, fry the curry leaves until they crackle. Mix
the leaves into the curry and serve.

GREEN MALLUM

MALLUM IS A COOKED SALAD; ANY BITTERISH GREENS WORK WELL. *Try turnip greens or radish or beet leaves. Everything must be finely shredded.*

> SERVES 6 AS PART OF A BIG SELECTION
> lemon, ½
> small red onion, very thinly sliced, *1*
> greens, very finely shredded, *1 pound*
> coconut, flesh grated (see page 73), ½
> fresh, hot green chile, deseeded and minced, *1*
> vegetable oil, *a small splash*

Squeeze the lemon juice over the onion, then mix with everything else except the oil. Heat a wide pan, pour in the oil, and add the greens mixture. Add some salt, then cook quickly until the greens have wilted and the flavors combined. Taste for salt and lemon juice, and serve at room temperature.

FRIED BITTER MELON
AND DRIED ANCHOVIES

BITTER MELON, IN ITS KNOBBLY GLORY, IS GREAT SALTED AND FRIED. *Should bitter melon be elusive, this also works with 2 zucchini or an eggplant.*

> SERVES 6 AS PART OF A BIG SELECTION
> Indian bitter melons, *2*
> ground turmeric, ¼ *teaspoon*
> dried anchovies, *4 ounces*
> vegetable oil, *for deep-frying*
> fresh curry leaves, *about 30*
> lemon, ½
> dried hot chile, crushed, *1*

Very thinly slice the bitter melons and put in a colander. Sprinkle with salt and the turmeric, then let drain while you soak the anchovies in warm water for 10 minutes. Heat about 2 inches of oil in a deep pot until almost smoking (360°F, if you have a thermometer). First fry the bitter melon until it's dark brown and crunchy. Put it on a plate lined with paper towels. Drain and dry the fish, then fry to a similar state and add to the bitter melon. Fry the curry leaves—they become translucent in seconds—and add to the bitter melon. Put the fried things in a bowl and sprinkle with lemon juice and chile. Taste: it should be strongly flavored. Eat it cold.

TOOR DHAL

THESE SPLIT YELLOW LENTILS GIVE THEIR NAME TO THE DISH.
The spice mixture makes enough to keep for another batch.

SERVES 6 AS PART OF A BIG SELECTION
for the spice mixture
coriander seeds, *3 tablespoons*
cumin seeds, *2 tablespoons*
fennel seeds, *1 tablespoon*
fenugreek seeds, *1 teaspoon*
cinnamon stick, *1½-inch piece*
green cardamom pods, seeds only, *10*
dried, long, mild red chile, *1*
black peppercorns, *1 heaping teaspoon*

for the dhal
yellow toor dhal or chana dhal, *1½ cups*
tomato, *1*
garlic cloves, halved and green shoot removed, *2*
sunflower oil, *1 tablespoon*
mustard seeds, *1 teaspoon*
dried, large red chile, *1*
fresh curry leaves, *20*

Toast the coriander, cumin, fennel, and fenugreek seeds separately in
a dry pan (they all toast at different rates—see Getting the Spice Right,
page 50). The cumin and coriander should be quite dark, but the fennel
and fenugreek just lightly toasted. Mix together in a mortar. Add the
rest of the spice mixture ingredients, then grind very fine with a pestle.

Rinse the dhal, tip into a pan, and cover with about 4 inches of cold
water. Drop in the whole tomato and the garlic. Bring to a boil, then
cover and simmer until completely soft, about 30 minutes for toor dhal,
or about 40 minutes for chana dhal. Add a little more water if the lentils
start to dry out. Add a heaping teaspoon of the spice mixture and a little
salt and cook for a few minutes longer, making sure the dhal remains
reasonably wet. Taste for spice mixture and salt, adding more of either
if you want.

Just before you eat, heat a frying pan and pour in the oil. When hot,
toss in the mustard seeds and chile. When the mustard crackles, add the
curry leaves. Immediately pour this onto the dhal. Serve warm.

GETTING THE SPICE RIGHT

Spices are incredible. I love to think of their history, imagining the rush to find a route to import exotic seeds, barks, and leaves from the East. I marvel at how chiles came first from Mexico to Portugal before they ever got to Thailand or India, and at the way peppercorns from Kerala have been so important on British tables for centuries.

When cooking with spices, it's all about balance. It takes a lot of experimentation, but, when you get the right mixture, the flavor of a dish suddenly takes on tangible authenticity, becoming immediately Moroccan, Kashmiri, or Sri Lankan. To achieve this you must learn the nature of each spice and, to be effective, it's important to use quite a lot.

Some seeds, such as cumin and coriander (which I think of as "dirty" spices), change when toasted. Always toast them individually, slowly in a dry pan, because all spices brown at their own rate and toasting to different levels affects the flavor of each considerably.

Sweet, fragrant spices like cardamom, cinnamon, cloves, and anise seed are seldom toasted and sit well in both sweet and savory recipes. They can be fabulous thrown into a pot of simmering rice or a delicate curry.

Grind spices yourself in a coarse-grained mortar and pestle, for the freshest possible aromas and maximum essential oils. These are lost in packages and jars of preground spice.

JOSEPH'S NONNA'S ORECCHIETTE

MY *friend Joseph has a grandmother from Campania who taught him to make orecchiette (little ears). He showed me and now I shall tell you. I imagine her when I make this pasta and propose a toast to her. Making it is simple, although I get people to help as it takes a while and you can do it sitting around the table.*

SERVES 2 FOR LUNCH OR 4 AS A FIRST COURSE

for the pasta
fine semolina flour for making pasta, *2 cups*
egg, *1*
fine salt, *a pinch*

for the sauce
broccoli, trimmed and cut into florets, *1 pound*
garlic clove, green sprout removed, thinly sliced, *1*
good olive oil, *generous slug*
salted anchovy fillets, *4 or 5*
fennel seeds, crushed, *1 teaspoon*
dried, small, hot chile, crushed, *1*

Pile up the semolina and make a well in the center. Crack in the egg and add the salt. Bring together with your hands, then knead until slightly elastic and smooth. Wrap in plastic and let sit while you make the sauce.

Boil the broccoli in salted water until soft. Fry the garlic gently in the oil; when it starts to brown, add the anchovies, fennel seeds, and chile and stir to melt the anchovy. Add the broccoli and a splash of its cooking water. Cook, breaking it up with your spoon, for 5 minutes, adding a splash of water when needed. The result should be a slightly oily, well-flavored sauce. Check the seasoning is bold and put it aside.

Roll the dough into sausages the width of a finger, then cut into playing dice. Using a table knife, squash and roll each into a curl, turning them inside out to make an ear. Try to make them thin. Boil in well-salted water until cooked but chewy, about 6 minutes. Mix with the sauce, then loosen with good oil and some cooking water, if needed.

TORTA DELLA NONNA

PROPER TORTA DELLA NONNA IS MORE CUSTARDY THAN MY VERSION.
Mine is more cheesecake-like, but fantastic nonetheless.

SERVES 6 – 8
ricotta, *1 cup*
sugar, *¾ cup*
egg yolks, *4*
heavy cream, *½ cup*
oranges, finely grated zest, *2*
lemons, finely grated zest and juice, *2*
10-inch sweet pastry shell, baked
   (see page 167), *1*
pine nuts, *a handful*

Preheat the oven to 325°F. Beat the ricotta, sugar, and yolks together. Stir in the cream, then the zests and juice.

Pour the mixture into the tart shell. Sprinkle with the pine nuts and bake until set and slightly brown, about 40 minutes. If it hasn't browned much, increase the oven temperature a bit at the end to give an appetizing color.

04

Spring has finally sprung, and it's a great time of year for picking the new shoots. So go foraging for leaves, fronds, and flowers to make tempura (see page 60). Eat your fill of asparagus, too, a more mainstream shoot, during its season (see page 56).

Celebrations and new beginnings seem perfectly placed in April as the new season gets underway. It's when we got engaged, and I give you the meal we ate to celebrate (see page 64). One of the things I love about cooking is that, with its evocative scents and tastes, a certain dish can immediately return you to a specific time and place. Food does this in a way that nothing else can.

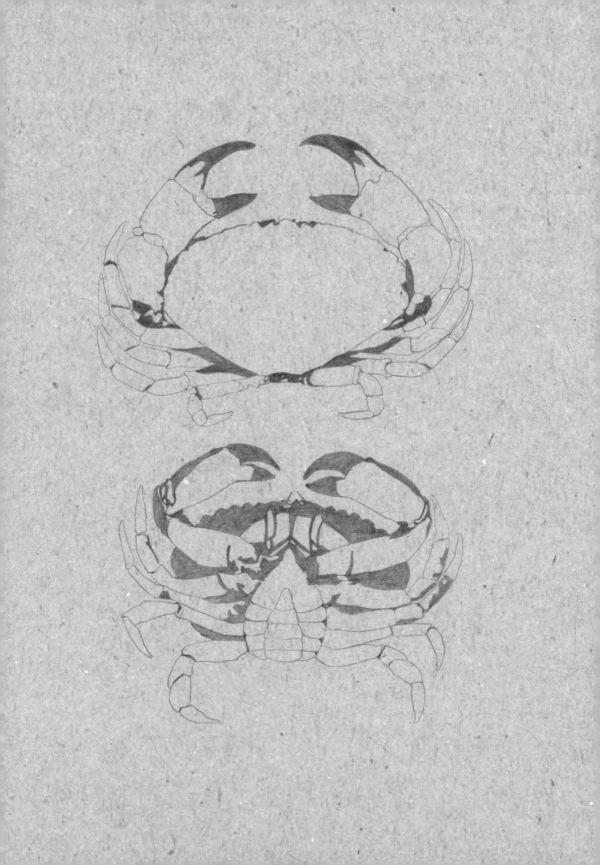

ASPARAGUS...

...is delicious, and locally grown asparagus the best of all. During its peak spring season you should make the most of it. I wait until the asparagus is really good—when it looks fresh and beautiful—before buying any. Look for plump, firm spears around ½ inch in diameter, with tight, slightly purplish heads.

Very thin asparagus spears are also wonderful and often cheaper. Just a glance at them explains why this vegetable is sometimes called "spaghetti grass." Use it in a different way: chop it up, and put it in soups.

Wild asparagus grows around the Mediterranean. I recall many an early summer vacation in Provence or Sicily, picking the first tiny wild stalks. Thrown onto a frying egg they make a most elegant breakfast and, being so thin, they cook in about the same time.

At the beginning of the season, I generally eat asparagus just blanched and dressed with butter (sometimes anchovies as well). As the season progresses I start to think of different recipes... and then, suddenly, the spears are gone for another year.

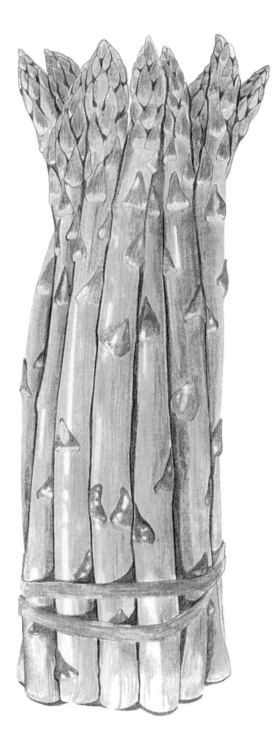

ASPARAGUS RISOTTO

CHOOSE YOUR PAN WITH CARE. EVERY RISOTTO NEEDS A GOOD PAN. *It should be high-sided and heavy-based for the best results. A long wooden spoon is essential, too.*

SERVES 4
butter, *⅔ cup (1¼ sticks)*
small red onion, minced, *1*
garlic cloves, green sprout removed, minced, *2*
thyme, *a few sprigs*
chicken stock, *8 cups*
asparagus, *1 bunch*
carnaroli or arborio rice, *2 heaping cups*
white wine (Soave or similar), *1¼ cups*
Parmesan, finely grated, *½ cup*

Melt most of the butter in your pan, reserving a tablespoon or so to add at the end. Tip in the onion, garlic, and thyme and add a generous amount of salt and pepper. Cook until the onion is softened, about 15 minutes. Put the stock on to boil.

Snap off the end of each asparagus spear; handily, it will break where it becomes tender. Discard the woody bases (or add them to the heating chicken stock for extra flavor). Now chop up all the asparagus. Don't do it too neatly—it should be rough with some bits bigger than others.

When the onion is really soft, add the asparagus. Increase the heat a little and stir to combine all the flavors. Now add the rice and stir until everything is well mixed and hot. If you put your ear close to the rice, you will hear that it has begun to "sing" a little as it sizzles. Pour in the wine and stir until it has evaporated.

Begin adding the hot stock, a ladleful at a time, stirring until it is all absorbed before adding another. All this stirring causes the risotto to become creamy, knocking starch off the rice without breaking it.

After about 20 minutes, taste a grain; it will probably still be hard in the middle. Adjust the salt and continue cooking and stirring. When the rice is almost completely translucent, with just a little white dot in the middle, remove from the heat. Add a bit more stock if the risotto is stodgy rather than glossy.

Stir in the remaining butter and the Parmesan. Don't worry about the asparagus not being bright green; the flavor will be better for the rice having spent so long in its company.

A KIND OF ROMAN EGGS MIMOSA

THIS IS HOW I WAS TAUGHT TO HARD-COOK EGGS BY M.F.K. FISHER. *I read about it in her book* How to Eat a Wolf. *If you have your preferred method for hard-cooking eggs, you should use it; the yolks must not be gray at the edges, nor the whites rubbery.*

FOR 2 AS A LOVELY LUNCH
OR 4 AS PART OF A FEAST
very fresh, good-quality, happy chicken's eggs, 2
salted capers, rinsed and minced, 1 *teaspoon*
flat-leaf parsley, minced, 1 *tablespoon*
aged pecorino, grated, *a handful*
good olive oil, *a splash*
asparagus, trimmed, 1 *bunch*
butter, *a walnut-sized piece*
lemon juice, *a squeeze*

Put the eggs in a pan, cover with cold water, and set the pan over medium heat, bringing the water to a boil. Ten minutes later, remove from the heat and let the eggs cool in the water. When the eggs are cool, peel them and grate coarsely. Gently mix with the capers, parsley, pecorino, and oil. (It is important to treat this mixture gently to avoid it becoming a paste.) Add seasoning; don't be shy with the black pepper.

Boil a pot of water that will easily accommodate your asparagus and season well with salt. Cook the asparagus until almost completely soft—it must have some resistance, but I think a crunch is unwelcome in the experience. About 6 minutes should do it.

Toss the hot asparagus with the little bit of butter, the lemon juice, and some seasoning, then serve with your egg sauce.

WILD TEMPURA

In early spring, around the time of the *sakura* (cherry blossom), the food shops in Tokyo start selling *sansai* (wild mountain vegetables). It was at this time of year that I visited the mountains near Kyoto. We stayed in a wooden house by a river. Just down the slope was a restaurant that used ingredients gathered in the mountains to make delicious, simple lunches: rice, wild tempura, and cooked, lightly pickled greens.

To recreate these meals is hard because the foraged ingredients are not available to us. So we must look closer to home, to find local wild flowers and greens that will tempura very nicely.

Even along the river by our houseboat in London we find delicious things. A very pretty little flower called marsh mallow deep-fries very nicely, especially if you pick the tops and get a clump of just-open buds. Wild fennel flowers, fronds, and seedheads definitely qualify. Mustard leaves, squash blossoms, and borage and chrysanthemum leaves and flowers are things you can forage from your own garden.

There are also everyday things that tempura well: asparagus, bell peppers, eggplant, carrots, Swiss chard, and squash. Fresh lotus root, which you can buy in any Chinatown, has an unusual, nutty flavor; rinse, then slice into thin wheels to tempura. Okra, left whole, is also lovely. It's important to get a considered mix of things to be fried, without too many of one or another.

The usual accompaniment is ten-tsuyu, a dashi (bonito and kelp stock) seasoned with vinegar and soy. It has the depth and delicacy always associated in my mind with Japanese cooking.

TO MAKE THE TEMPURA BATTER

TEMPURA BATTER IS VERY SIMPLE TO MAKE, SO YOU SHOULD TRY IT. *You can use special tempura flour, but I think this mixture of all-purpose flour and cornstarch gives excellent results.*

MAKES ABOUT ENOUGH FOR TEMPURA FOR 2
all-purpose flour, *1⅓ cups*
cornstarch, *2 tablespoons*

Put the flour and cornstarch in a mixing bowl and slowly add about 1 cup ice water, using chopsticks to whisk. When the mixture forms a paste, whisk away well to work out any lumps. Then continue to pour in the water, still whisking, until the batter is as thick as heavy cream. Dip in your finger to check the consistency; it should delicately but resiliently coat. If it doesn't, you may need a little more water.

TEN-TSUYU (DIPPING SAUCE)

YOU CAN BUY DASHI IN JAPANESE MARKETS AND SUPERMARKETS.

SERVES 2
dashi, *¾ cup*
shoyu or tamari (Japanese soy sauce), *about 2 tablespoons*
mirin (Japanese rice vinegar), *about 2 tablespoons*

Warm the dashi, then season delicately, tasting all the time, with soy and vinegar. You will know when you have it right—it quite magically achieves that deep but delicate Japanese balance.

PREPARING THE
TEMPURA VEGETABLES

When you have gathered your shoots and leaves, or bought your relevant supplies—or both—lay them all out and take a view. Imagine eating them, and come up with the best selection and way to cut them.

Winter and summer squashes and eggplant need to be sliced thinly. Okra must be left whole. Squash blossoms need to have the furry inside stamen removed. Any shoots and leaves you have foraged must be carefully examined for any hard stalks or insects. Everything must be ready to cook and then eat.

FRYING

You should have a pan about 10 inches wide and deep enough to allow the oil to triple in volume and not overflow, which would cause a terrible mess at best.

Heat the oil to 360°F. If you don't have a thermometer, this is very hot but not smoking—a drop of batter should fizzle gently and rise immediately to the surface of the oil.

Put your vegetables into the batter, a few pieces at a time, and mix them about, making sure each piece is thinly coated. Fry them without crowding the pan, letting the batter crisp but not to brown. Remove and lay on paper towels to blot off excess oil while you cook the next few pieces. Work quickly so you can eat all your tempura hot.

Eat them with chopsticks, dipping each piece into the warmed sauce.

Do try…

Making tempura with fresh corn kernels cut off the cob. Make the batter with an added egg yolk and mix enough of this into the corn to lightly coat. Spoon the battered kernels into the hot oil in long, loose clusters. Season after frying with a little salt instead of ten-tsuyu.

CHAMPAGNE, CRAB, AND FAVA BEANS.

CELEBRATING OUR ENGAGEMENT

W HEN *Nicky and I decided to get married, we celebrated with—of course—a lovely meal. There is nothing better than sharing food and moments with friends. We felt very lucky not only to have a grand Champagne from Krug, but also a big crab... and the first, tiny fava beans of the year, just picked on our floating pontoon vegetable garden from the* acquadulce *plants we had planted in the autumn. And of course we had to have ice cream (see page 66).*

FAVA BEANS AND PECORINO

Picked while still soft and very tender, young fava beans are at their most delicious raw. Serve them in an enormous pile with a big wedge of aged, salty sheep's cheese next to them.

KAMPOT PEPPER CRAB AND JASMINE RICE

A FAVORITE OF OURS. I FOUND IT WHILE TRAVELING IN CAMBODIA. *I was 16, slightly mad, and always looking for delicious food even then. Years later, I took Nicky to taste it, when it was cooked by an old lady on a white beach. Kampot is famous for its pepper. The fairly large quantity of fresh green peppercorns in this recipe (find them in good Thai markets) really makes the dish. If you can only find those that come in brine, rinse them very well.*

SERVES 4

medium, live crabs, *2*
vegetable oil, *¼ cup*
fresh green peppercorns on the vine, *10 strands*
scallions, whites minced, green roughly chopped, *4*
fresh ginger, thinly sliced, *1-inch piece*
big garlic cloves, green sprout removed, roughly chopped, *3*
big ripe tomatoes (canned and rinsed are fine), *6*
oyster sauce, *¼ cup*
light soy sauce, *¼ cup*
palm sugar or brown sugar, *2 teaspoons*
limes, *5*

Put the crabs belly up on a board. Insert a skewer just above the tail flap. They will die instantly. Smash the claws a bit and cut the bodies in half.

Heat the oil until almost smoking in a large wok or saucepan. Put in the crab to frazzle for a couple of minutes, then add the peppercorns, scallions, ginger, and garlic. Continue cooking and stirring until the pepper is fragrant and the garlic light brown. Squeeze and tear up the tomatoes, then throw them into the wok. After 30 seconds, add the oyster sauce, soy sauce, and palm sugar. Stir and toss to mix.

Reduce the heat and put on the lid to allow the crab to steam for a few more minutes, to be sure it is cooked through. Add a splash of water if it looks like it might burn. When it's ready, the meat should pull away easily—check the meat inside the largest claw. Squeeze in lime juice to taste and serve with a big pile of jasmine rice.

JASMINE RICE Rinse about ½ cup rice per person until the water runs clear without any milkiness. Drain and place in a deep pot. Add enough water to cover plus ¾ inch. Bring to a boil, then reduce the heat to very low, cover, and simmer until cooked, about 20 minutes. Remove from the heat and let sit, still covered, for at least 10 minutes. Fluff up the grains with chopsticks or a fork before serving.

MASALA ICE CREAM

ICE CREAM IS DEFINITELY MY FAVORITE SWEET THING OF THEM ALL. *And, for a celebration, it is brilliant and immensely satisfying to make. You can either churn it in a machine or freeze it in molds, when it becomes icy like the Indian ice cream, kulfi. Gum arabic (or mastic), which is the sap of a sub-Saharan tree, is used to change the texture of lots of Arab sweets. It makes the ice cream more chewy and is an exotic addition, which I like.*

SERVES 4–6
whole milk, *2 quarts*
heavy cream, *1 cup*
green cardamom pods, *2 handfuls*
black peppercorns, *1 teaspoon*
cinnamon stick, *a small piece*
cloves, *2*
star anise, *1*
whole almonds, *a handful*
gum arabic (optional), *1 teaspoon*
rosewater, *⅔ cup*
sugar, *¾–1 cup*

Put all the ingredients except the rosewater and sugar in a heavy-based pot. Simmer very gently, stirring often, on the lowest possible heat—use a heat diffuser, if possible—until reduced by two-thirds, and thick and yellow. This will take a couple of hours. Be careful not to burn the mixture; if it starts to stick to the bottom of the pot, pour it out and clean the pot before continuing. If it does actually burn, start again.

Add the rosewater and sugar to taste, remembering that once frozen the ice cream will seem less sweet and aromatic. Strain out the flavorings and chill well, then churn, or freeze it in molds.

DEEP-FRYING DELICATELY

Deep-frying has a bad reputation. But when performed carefully, it is an excellent and delicate way to cook. The ingredient is enclosed in a complete seal and cooked incredibly quickly at a very high temperature. The true flavor of the food is preserved and, with a little salt, the (hopefully) crisp batter is delicious.

The masters of deep-frying are the Japanese. Tempura (see page 62) is a lesson in delicacy, and the traditional accompaniments make a perfect combination.

There are different types of batter from all cuisines, made from varying ingredients. But whether an English beer batter, an Italian fritto misto coating, or a Japanese tempura, its consistency is always critical. Too thick and it will be a claggy, stodgy affair; too thin and the food will not be properly sealed in its protective coat. The best way to test if a batter has the right consistency is to dip your finger into it. The batter should coat your finger well, but you should be able to make out your knuckles and nail.

The other important thing is the heat of the oil. It must be hot enough for the batter to seal quickly and not absorb oil, but not so hot that the batter browns too quickly and the food inside burns. Test the temperature with a special thermometer, or by dropping a piece of batter into the oil: it should rise immediately to the surface and sizzle.

I prefer to flour some foods rather than coating in batter, to give a crunchier, harder exterior. Pieces of artichoke are delicious dipped into milk and then into semolina flour before being fried. The milk, which helps the flour to stick, works better than water, because it adds a little sugar so the artichoke will brown as it fries.

05

May heralds another short but exciting season, that of the
Alphonso mango from India (see page 70). Eat as many as you
can while they are around. Yogurt and mango go incredibly well
together, especially if you make your own yogurt, which tends to
have a more vibrant acidity (see page 72). If you make yogurt to go
with your mango and have some left over, add a little salt, toasted
cumin, and chilled water for a delicious savory lassi.

This month gives the first opportunity of the year for comfortable
outdoor pursuits. Being such a city boy, my picnics tend to take
place in urban parks. A pork pie wrapped in a dish towel, a bottle
of beer, and a pot of good Dijon mustard is certainly all I need
(see page 78).

DELICIOUS INDIAN MANGOES

All through April and May, my eyes stray to the front stalls of local ethnic markets, searching for gaudy boxes of Alphonso mangoes from Maharashtra. They really are amazing, beautifully yellow-skinned, orange-fleshed, and full of miraculous nectar that drips down your chin and immediately transports you to the side of a dusty Indian road.

The season for the Alphonso is short (about five weeks) but, as it goes out, the larger Kesar mango comes in. Hailing from farther north, it is a little larger, paler in color, and more delicate in flavor, a welcome change from the headily intense Alphonso. There is a steady stream of different varieties for a month or two because each area of India and Pakistan has their own mango. Good ripe mangoes are best eaten alone, although under-ripe, sour mangoes have more creative culinary uses, such as in a fresh pickle (see page 72) or a curry (see page 73).

CHOOSING MANGOES

Mangoes ripen well off the tree. Therefore, choose your mango not just for its ripeness but also for its beauty. Smooth, unwrinkled, unbruised skin with no discoloration or blemishes is what you want. I always buy yellow Indian or Pakistani mangoes—the bigger green mangoes from South America may look tempting, but, in my opinion, they are simply not as nice.

HOW TO CUT A FRESH MANGO

I love to cut a mango in the way my grandfather taught me.

1. First slice the two flatter sides of the mango away from the large pit.

2. Now, with a table knife, score the flesh right down to the skin into crosshatched squares.

3. Turn each half mango inside out, and cut off the cubes with a knife.
    Eat it with some yogurt.

FRESH MANGO PICKLE

SLIGHTLY UNDER-RIPE MANGO MAKES THE PICKLE PROPERLY ZINGY. *Eat this with a plain piece of white fish and greens. It keeps a few days, tightly covered, in the refrigerator.*

MAKES A SMALL BOWLFUL
under-ripe mango, *1*
oil, *2 tablespoons*
mustard seeds, *½ teaspoon*
ground turmeric, *¼ teaspoon*
black pepper, *¼ teaspoon*
mild chile powder, such as Kashmiri, *½ teaspoon*
asafetida, *a pinch*
lemon, *1*

Very finely dice the mango flesh. Heat the oil in a small pan and add the mustard seeds. When they crackle, add the turmeric, pepper, chile, and asafetida, then throw in the mango. Let the mango quickly frizzle. Tip everything into a bowl. Season with salt. Taste and adjust the seasoning with lemon juice. Remember that this pickle's role is to lift the flavors of other things, so make sure it's acidic, sweet, and spicy.

HOW TO MAKE YOGURT

MANGOES AND YOGURT ARE EACH OTHER'S PERFECT COMPLEMENT. *Both of the mango recipes here benefit from being served with a bowl of your own yogurt. To make your first batch, you will need to buy some live yogurt. After that, you can use your own. After a few weeks, your yogurt might stop working well or may get quite strong; if this happens start again with more purchased live yogurt. Try to find unpasteurized milk for the best results.*

MAKES ABOUT 2 CUPS
whole milk, *2 cups*
live yogurt, *¼ cup*

Scald the milk (be careful not to burn it), then transfer it to a heavy earthenware bowl so it will keep its heat. When it has cooled to a little warmer than body temperature, stir in the yogurt. Cover with plastic wrap, wrap in a dish towel, and leave somewhere warm overnight. The next day, put it in the refrigerator.

SOUR MANGO CURRY

YOU CAN USE ANY SMALL GREEN MANGO, AS LONG AS IT IS SOUR.
The dish is good with a Chapati (see page 10), or rice, and a sweeter curry, such as Okra with Tomatoes (see page 111). You'll need a whole coconut to make the coconut milk for the curry (see below). It really is worth the bother.

SERVES 4
small, green mangoes, diced, *2*
garlic cloves, green sprout removed, minced, *2*
mustard seeds, ground with a squeeze of lemon, *4 teaspoons*
second-extract coconut milk (see below), *2 cups*
mild chile powder, *1 teaspoon*
fresh ginger, minced, *½-inch piece*
cinnamon stick, *¾-inch piece*
fresh, small, red chile, minced, *1*
black pepper, *¼ teaspoon*
ground cumin, *½ teaspoon*
first-extract coconut milk (see below), *½ cup*

Put all the ingredients, except the first-extract coconut milk, in a pan.
Add salt, and cook over medium heat until the mango is soft. Stir in the thick first-extract coconut milk and serve.

HOW TO MAKE LABNE

A DRAINED, THICK AND CREAMY ARAB-STYLE YOGURT.

Season your homemade yogurt well with salt, then pour it into a bowl lined with a clean dish towel. Tie up the towel and place it in a strainer set over the bowl. Let drain somewhere cool overnight. You can dip flatbread or crudités into the labne, and it is especially good with a dried anchovy fillet or two placed on top.

TO MAKE FRESH COCONUT MILK

Hold a coconut in your left hand and hit it with the blunt side of a heavy knife all the way around the circumference. Make sure you do this over a bowl to collect the coconut water. (If the coconut smells bad inside, throw it away.) When you have two halves of coconut, smash or prize the flesh from the shell. Peel and grate the flesh. Put it into a bowl and pour in ½ cup boiling water. Leave until cool enough to handle, then squeeze the milk from it handful by handful over a strainer. This thick milk is the first extraction. Put the grated coconut back into the bowl. Pour 2 cups boiling water over it, mix, and leave it for a couple of minutes. Drain through the strainer, pushing and squeezing out all the liquid. This is the second extraction. Keep these two coconut milks separate.

A REAL TREAT.
A GIFT OF FRESH MORELS

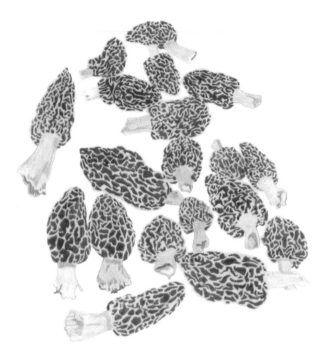

Morels are a beautiful and rare spring mushroom. Tall and magical, they are so astonishing to look at that you can almost imagine little pixies sleeping beneath them. Surprisingly, they grow prolifically in the foothills of the Himalayas. In Kashmir, they make a delicious rice dish with basmati, wild black cumin, and these precious mushrooms (see opposite). The flavor is perfect with the delicate spices.

I was delighted when my friend Tom brought me some he had picked himself in the woods not far from Glasgow. I was also jealous, because I have never found them. I sometimes use dried morels (or even porcini) for this biriani, if the fresh mushrooms are out of season or simply hiding from me too successfully.

MOREL AND BLACK CUMIN BIRIANI

A LUXURIOUS AND EXOTIC DISH FOR A VERY SPECIAL MUSHROOM.
The rice is infused with the flavor of the morel, and the cumin goes so nicely. If you don't have fresh morels, use 2 ounces dried morels, soaked to rehydrate.

SERVES 4
basmati rice, *2 heaping cups*
fresh morels, *7 ounces*
butter, *7 tablespoons*
onions, thinly sliced into half-moons, *2*
garlic cloves, green sprout removed, chipped, *2*
cloves, *4*
green cardamom pods, *6*
cinnamon stick, *1-inch piece*
allspice berries, crushed, *1 teaspoon*
black cumin, *1 heaping teaspoon*
dill, chopped, *a few sprigs*
parsley, chopped, *a few sprigs*
mint, chopped, *a few leaves*

Soak the rice in water. Clean the morels with a brush, then tear them in half and carefully remove any woody parts with a knife.

Choose a high-sided, thick-bottomed pan, similar to one you would use for risotto. Melt the butter and fry the onions very gently with the garlic and all the spices until really soft, about 20 minutes, stirring occasionally so nothing sticks to the pan. Season well with salt.

Drain the rice. Increase the heat under the onions, add the morels, and cook for a couple of minutes longer. Tip in the rice and stir to combine, then cook until the rice is hot, 2–3 minutes. Pour in enough boiling water to cover the rice plus about ¾ inch. Cover with a piece of parchment paper and the lid. Cook on high heat for 3–4 minutes, then reduce the heat and cook for 5 minutes longer. Remove from the heat and let sit, still covered and undisturbed, for 10 minutes.

Fluff the herbs into the rice with a fork. Serve with a little yogurt (see page 72), if you fancy it.

PEAS AND MORELS

EARLY PEAS WITH MORELS ARE DELICIOUSLY SWEET AND EARTHY. *This is great with a delicate fish such as trout (see right). Because of the recipe's simplicity, you really do need to use a really good butter.*

SERVES 2
small, young onions, finely sliced, *2*
butter, *¼ cup (½ stick)*
thyme, *2 sprigs*
fresh morels, *4 ounces*
fresh peas, shelled, *2 cups*
chervil, chopped, *a few sprigs*

Fry the onions gently in the butter with the thyme leaves picked from the stem. Clean the morels with a brush and cut the tough end from the bottom, being careful not to waste any. Add the morels to the onion and then the peas. Cook gently, covered with a piece of parchment paper and the lid, adding a tiny bit of water if the peas become too dry. Cook until the peas are tender, then add the chervil. Eat with your fish (see right) and some boiled new potatoes, or some baby romaine leaves with a good vinaigrette.

A BAKED FISH

I HAD A BEAUTIFUL FRESH WILD BROWN TROUT. I WAS DELIGHTED. *They are best in late spring and early summer, which coincides with the season for morels. You could use another wild trout or even a good farm-raised rainbow trout if a wild brown trout eludes you. For the herbs, use a few sprigs of thyme, bay, rosemary, or fennel—whatever you have growing or in the refrigerator.*

SERVES 2
a fish, *2¼ pounds*
herbs, *a few sprigs*
butter, *a few walnut-sized pieces*
lemon, *1*

Preheat the oven to its hottest setting. Loosely lay a piece of foil on a baking sheet. Put your fish on this and tuck the herbs in, on, and around him. Put the pieces of butter on top. Squeeze the juice from the lemon over and put the squeezed fruit next to the fish. Scrunch up the foil around the fish to keep the juices close by. Season the skin and inside the cavity.

Bake your fish until it is cooked, about 15 minutes, depending on how hot your oven is. You can test for doneness by pushing a skewer through the flesh and seeing how much resistance there is—with an undercooked fish, you can feel the spike going through the layers of flesh. I think it's nice to eat wild trout and salmon slightly undercooked.

A PERFECT PICNIC WITH HOMEMADE PORK PIE AND A POT OF DIJON

PORK *pie—a self-contained meal—is really very good for a picnic. It feels special to be setting off on a hike with a handsome pie wrapped up in a dish towel. And if you have a few bottles of ale and a jar of mustard, a blanket, and a pretty girl, what could be better? People have some reservations about the aspic in a pork pie, but it is important as a complement to the pastry and the rich meat. I think the aspic also helps the pie to keep a little longer, because it fills in all the air pockets between pork and pastry. Hyssop and savory are wonderful old-fashioned herbs, but unless you grow them yourself (which I would recommend) you won't find them, so you can use more thyme instead.*

MAKES AN 8-INCH PIE

for the aspic
pig's foot, *1*
pork bones, *1½ pounds*
cloves, *2*
onion, *¼*
juniper berries, *4*
carrot, *1*
black peppercorns, *25*

for the hot-water pastry
unsalted butter, *6 tablespoons*
lard, *7 tablespoons*
fine salt, *1 heaping teaspoon*
all-purpose flour, *4 cups*

for the filling
boned pork shoulder, coarsely
   ground, *1 pound*
boned pork shoulder, cut into
   ½-inch dice, *8 ounces*
Canadian bacon, cut into ½-inch
   pieces, *4 ounces*
thyme, minced, *a few sprigs*
sage, minced, *a few sprigs*
hyssop, minced, *a few sprigs*
savory, minced, *a few sprigs*
nutmeg

for the egg wash
egg yolks, *2*
milk, *¼ cup*

Put all the ingredients for the aspic into a big pot, cover with water, and bring to a boil. Simmer for 3 hours. Strain, then boil again until reduced to about 2 cups. Set aside.

For the pastry, pour ½ cup boiling water over the butter and lard in a small saucepan. Add the salt and heat just until everything has melted. Put the flours in a mixing bowl and pour in the hot fat mixture. Mix with a knife until cool enough to handle, then use your hands to bring the dough into a ball. Put in a clean bowl and leave until cold and firm.

Combine the ground and diced pork and bacon. Season with salt and lots of pepper. Add the herbs and grate in a little nutmeg. Mix well. Make a tiny burger from a little of the meat and cook in a hot pan, then taste to check the seasoning; the pepper should give a little spice. Don't be tempted (as I often am) to add too many flavorings.

Roll out the pastry dough on a well-floured surface to about ¾ inch thick. (Dust with flour and fold into a square to make it easier to roll; if the pastry is still sticky, roll out and fold again.) Take one-third and roll it out into a circle a little larger than the base of an 8-inch springform cake pan. Set this aside for the top crust. Roll out the remaining pastry into a big round just under ¾ inch thick. Lay this in the pan to line it, pushing the pastry into the corners and patching any holes. Cut off any excess pastry, leaving a lip hanging over the rim all around. Put the filling into the pastry shell and push it down so there are no gaps. Lay the top crust in place and crimp the edges together to seal.

Cut a ¾-inch hole in the top crust. Cover the hole with a small piece of pastry. Let the pie rest in the refrigerator for an hour or two.

Preheat the oven to 350°F. Carefully remove the pie from the pan and set it on a baking sheet. It will probably settle a bit during baking, and the sides will bulge out, but it should survive.

Beat the yolks and milk together. Paint this all over the pie, to give a glossy look. Bake to give the pastry a good color, about 30 minutes, then reduce the heat to 300°F. Continue baking for 1½ hours. If the pastry gets too brown, reduce the heat further. When the pie is done, remove the square of pastry covering the hole and let cool.

Gently warm the aspic to make it liquid again. Put it into a pitcher and very slowly pour it into the hole in the top crust. It will fill the gaps left by the shrinking of the cooked meat. When the pie is full of aspic, cover the hole once more and let set for at least a few hours.

Wrap in a dish towel and take on your hike. Don't forget the mustard.

FIVE DEVELOPMENT STUDENTS AND ONE SOMMELIER FOR A MIDDLE-EASTERN VEGETABLE SUPPER

*A*N *unusual combination of people, they are now dispersed all over the world. It was a pleasure to enjoy their extraordinary conversation. In my left ear I was hearing how to save the world through economics, while in the right I got a lesson on which wine was corked and what that means anyway.*

COUSCOUS WITH FAVA BEANS

A DELICIOUS MIXTURE THAT MAKES AN EXCELLENT BREAKFAST.
Here it worked well as part of a mixed table.

SERVES 4
small fresh fava beans, shelled, *8 ounces*
fine couscous (not the coarse or pre-cooked stuff), *1 heaping cup*
olive oil
small spring garlic clove, *1*
cumin seeds, *1 teaspoon*
thin, plain yogurt, preferably homemade (see page 72), *¼ cup*
cilantro leaves, chopped, *2 tablespoons*

Briefly boil the beans in unsalted water (salt toughens the skins), then place in a bowl with the couscous. Sprinkle with salt and 1 tablespoon olive oil. Rub everything between your hands to coat in oil. Pour in enough hot water to cover, then leave until it has been absorbed, about 15 minutes.

Crush the garlic with salt to a fine paste. Toast the cumin seeds in a dry pan. When they crackle, grind with the garlic in a mortar and pestle, adding the yogurt and some black pepper. Mix the couscous with the yogurt and cilantro, and check the seasoning. Drizzle a little more olive oil over the top.

EGGPLANT, WALNUTS, MINT, AND YOGURT

THIS IS MY FAVORITE DISH IN OUR LOCAL PERSIAN RESTAURANT.
It's great as a dip. I generally eat it all, much to the dismay of my wife, Nicky.

SERVES 4 AS PART OF A SPREAD
large eggplants, *2*
spring garlic clove, *1*
mint leaves, *a few*
walnut halves, *30*
olive oil, *¼ cup*
white Arab cheese or feta, *2 ounces*
lemon, *1*

Grill the eggplants whole over hot coals, or under the broiler, until the skin is black and the eggplant has almost collapsed. This will take about 20 minutes. Put in a colander to cool. Crush the garlic in a mortar and pestle. Add the mint and then the nuts, crushing to a paste. Add the oil and cheese, and mash everything up until smooth. When the eggplants are cool, remove the skin and put the flesh in a bowl. Add the walnut mixture. Squeeze in the lemon juice and mix, squashing the eggplants to a smooth mush. Taste for balance and salt. Eat at room temperature.

PEAS WITH ALLSPICE

DELICIOUS FRESH PEAS ARE VERY WELCOME AS PART OF THE MEZZE.
Make sure you cook them until they are soft.

SERVES 4 AS PART OF A SPREAD
butter, *¼ cup (½ stick)*
red onion, minced, *1*
garlic cloves, sliced, *2*
ground allspice, *1 teaspoon*
fresh peas, shelled, *2¼ pounds*
cilantro leaves, *a handful*

Melt the butter in a pan and add the onion, garlic, and allspice. Cover and cook gently, stirring occasionally, until the onion is soft and sweet, about 15 minutes. Add the peas and cilantro. Cover with a circle of parchment paper and the lid. Cook gently, adding a splash of water and stirring occasionally, until the peas are soft; this will take 10–15 minutes. Mush them up a little and season well.

HERBS AND CHEESE (PANEER SABZI)

THE IMPORTANT THING HERE IS TO USE THE FRESHEST HERBS.
I tend to use those I've grown myself and soak them in cold water to crisp up. Use a good balance of herbs—at least three, in about equal quantities—but be sure to include tarragon.

SERVES 4 AS PART OF A SPREAD
any of the following herbs: tarragon, mint, holy basil, flat-leaf parsley, marjoram, fennel fronds, *8 ounces in total*
breakfast radishes (or red globe) with leaves, *a few*
walnut halves, *a handful*
white Arab cheese or feta, *3 ounces*

Soak the whole sprigs of herbs, radishes, and walnuts in water. Dry them carefully in a clean, soft dish towel.

Put the herbs in a big pile with the cheese, walnuts, and radishes next to them. Eat a bit of each, wrapped up in a warm piece of flatbread. It really is very delicious.

SEMOLINA DOUGH FLATBREAD

MAKES 10 FLATBREADS
active dry yeast, *2 teaspoons*
fine semolina flour for pasta, *8 cups*
olive oil, *½ cup*
fine salt, *2 teaspoons*

Sprinkle the yeast over ½ cup of lukewarm water; it should all dissolve into a smooth liquid.

Put the semolina, oil, and salt in a bowl and add the yeasty water. Mix to bring the ingredients together, adding more water until you have a sticky, thick dough. Work it with your hands, pushing and pulling until it's stretchy and more glossy. Add a little more semolina, if needed, until it no longer feels sticky. Let rest for an hour or so in a bowl tightly covered with plastic wrap.

Form the dough into golfball-sized spheres. Roll them out into ¼-inch-thick disks. Let rest for about 15 minutes, covered with a damp cloth.

Preheat the oven to 425°F. Bake the flatbreads until firm and lightly golden brown, 5–10 minutes. Eat quickly.

BAKED LOQUATS

WE SEE THESE FRUITS IN MIDDLE-EASTERN SHOPS IN LATE SPRING. *In Italy, they are called* nespole, *in France* nefle; *Japanese medlar or plum are other names. Japan produces the most, but they are also grown in North and South America and in Israel. Many people don't know what to do with them. When ripe and sweet they are delicious eaten fresh; however, those I buy are often a little under-ripe, so I bake them with almonds and rosewater.*

Preheat the oven to 350°F. Cut the loquats in half and remove the small hard seeds from the center, pulling out any sinewy bits as well.

Put the loquats in a baking dish and mix with a good sprinkling of sugar, a splash of rosewater, and some coarsely crushed, blanched almonds. Bake until they are a little tiny bit black and mostly soft, about 15 minutes. Eat with yogurt or crème fraîche.

Junc is one of my favorite months in which to cook, because it's
so loaded with luxury for our kitchens. There's great produce all
around us and the first of the summer stone fruits starts to arrive
as a wonderful treat. They are always welcome in my home, going
into baking (see page 92) and cocktails (see page 93), or even given
as gifts at breakfast time (see page 89).

The garlic is fairly well developed at this time of year, and it's a
great time to think again about the bulb. Garlic is such a familiar
item in everyone's kitchen that we may feel we already know it
inside out. But one of the important things in cooking—and the
thing that makes a good cook great—is the ability to step back and
think about the fundamentals of any one ingredient. Sometimes a
new approach to the basics, such as garlic (see page 86), can yield
a whole new array of tastes.

GARLIC IS AMAZING.

So many flavors can be achieved by treating garlic in subtly different ways. How it is cut and when it is added can dramatically alter a dish. It can be sweet or bitter, round a recipe off, or drown out other flavors. I seem to be constantly learning.

At different times of year, garlic is different. In spring, the skin is soft and moist—just peel away a few layers and slice the bulb as you would an onion. Its flavor is delicate, so I tend to use a bigger quantity more recklessly.

1. All too soon, however, garlic changes and a little green sprout appears inside.

2. Always slice the clove in half lengthwise and remove this, because it has a horrible flavor.

Now decide how to cut it. Different dishes need different cuts. Small pieces burn easily and burned garlic is to be avoided. **So experiment.**

3. *Try using very even, thinly sliced garlic at the beginning of a tomato sauce.*

Watch it change as it cooks; it has different stages as it frazzles and new tastes for each stage. Initially it's pungent, then it becomes sweeter. It has a stage where it's sticky, then it develops bitterness as it browns. For a second it's deliciously nutty, then suddenly it's burned and you have to throw it away.

4. *Add minced garlic to a really hot pan of mushrooms or zucchini.*

5. *Use little chips in long-cooked dishes and in Indian food, when you want to keep its separate identity.*

Crushed raw garlic is the bulb at its most potent. I crush it in a mortar and pestle with quite a lot of salt until smooth, then add it sparingly to raw sauces. **I mean really sparingly**—sometimes just half a clove in 30 portions of sauce can have a very strong flavor.

AJO BLANCO—A BEAUTIFUL AND DELICATE SPANISH LUNCH.

I MAKE THIS AS SOON AS THE FIRST CHARENTAIS MELONS ARRIVE.
It is important to try to buy really good almonds. The best I have found are the rounder nuts grown in Valencia, Marcona, or Puglia; the thinner and longer almonds don't have the same perfumed flavor. Traditionally this soup is very garlicky, although I add a little bit less than the average señora. As with many of the things I cook, the process is very important to me. I love to grind this soup until smooth in my big granite mortar and pestle. When melons are out of season I make this with grapes or, in the fall, little bits of apple.

SERVES 4
garlic clove, green sprout removed, ½
whole almonds, blanched, 1½ *cups*
very stale bread, ½ *slice*
olive oil, *a few tablespoons*
sherry vinegar, *about 1 tablespoon*
Charentais or other cantaloupe melon, 1

In a large mortar and pestle, crush the garlic with a big pinch of coarse salt until completely smooth. Add the almonds and continue to bash and grind. It's best to get the almonds really fine at this point, before you start adding the liquid. Add the bread (put it in the oven to dry out if it is at all soft) and continue to grind. Add some olive oil, about the same amount of water, and the vinegar. The paste will become a little looser and you will be able to continue to grind until it is completely smooth. Slowly add water while grinding until the mixture is the thickness of heavy cream. Taste and adjust the salt and acidity.

Cut the melon in half, discard the seeds, and scoop out the flesh, getting about four big curls of melon from each half. Put a couple into each bowl and pour the ajo blanco over. Drizzle a little olive oil on top.

A VISITING IRISH ANGEL MADE US BREAKFAST.

MY *great friend Gillian Hegarty is a fabulous cook and an indefatigable person. When she came to visit in June, we awoke to find the boat ship-shape and this in my kitchen. She—of course—had gone off sky-diving or something. This is how she made it (I think).*

APRICOTS BAKED WITH SAUTERNES

SERVES 4
apricots, halved, *10*
sugar, *5 tablespoons*
Sauternes or similar sweet wine, *1 cup*

Preheat the oven to 300°F. Put the apricots in a baking dish and add the sugar and wine. Bake until soft, about 10 minutes.

CUSTARD POTS

SERVES 4
milk, *1 cup*
heavy cream, *1 cup*
vanilla bean, *1*
egg yolks, *4*
sugar, *½ cup*

Preheat the oven to 300°F. Put the milk and cream in a small pan. Slit the vanilla bean open and scrape the seeds into the pan. Heat gently until almost boiling. Whisk the yolks with the sugar. Pour in the hot cream mixture, whisking until smooth. Pour into little pots or custard cups. Set in a pan of water that comes two-thirds of the way up the sides of the pots. Bake until set, about 30 minutes.

CHERRIES

I adore cherry trees. Their beautiful blossoms herald the coming spring and their delicious fruit is the first of the real summer. When I lived in Japan, it seemed the whole year was geared up just to see the *sakura* (cherry blossoms). "Golden Week" is the only national holiday of the year, and it is celebrated with *hanami* (cherry-blossom-watching) parties. People camp out under the best trees and, when night falls, they light lanterns and sit there drinking, talking, and watching the blossoms fall. It seems only right that such a fleetingly beautiful blossom should produce such a fine and tempting fruit. From the black, gum-dying Provençal cherries to the mouth-scrunchingly sour Morello, all are welcome at my table or in my pot.

One of my favorite cocktails is a cherry-based drink, using Maraschino cherry liqueur. The "Aviation," which was introduced to me by my friend Claire "Cakes" Ptak of Violet Cakes, is responsible for many a sore head. A delicious drink nonetheless, zingy and appealing—dangerously so.

CHERRY FOCACCIA

IN JUNE IN FLORENCE, THIS CHERRY FOCACCIA IS ALL THE RAGE.
*It's difficult to give a recipe for bread, as quantities are really in the hands of
the baker, so just use this as a guide. The result you want is a dough that feels
soft and luxurious.*

MAKES 1 LOAF
fresh yeast, *about ¾ ounce*
"00" pasta flour or all-purpose flour, *4 cups*
salt, *a generous pinch*
sugar, *a generous pinch*
olive oil
cherries, pitted, *40*
fennel seeds, crushed, *a sprinkling*
rosemary leaves, chopped, *a sprinkling*

Dissolve the yeast in ½ cup lukewarm water. Make a pile of the flour
and dig a well in the center. Add the salt and sugar.

Using medium-good olive oil with a slow pourer, pour oil onto the
flour for 10 seconds. It seems a lot, but this will give the focaccia the rich
shortness it needs. Add the yeasty water, then bring the dough together,
adding more water as necessary to make a loose, stretchy, soft dough.
Knead well. Place the dough in a bowl, cover with plastic wrap, and let
rise in a warm place.

After an hour or so, when the dough has risen nicely, turn it out onto
a baking sheet and push it with your hands to make a thin focaccia.
Push the cherries into the top. Sprinkle with fennel seeds, rosemary, a
little more salt and sugar, and a generous drizzle of olive oil. Push your
fingers into the dough to make dimples to catch the juice. Cover with
plastic wrap again and let rise a little more (about half an hour if it
is a warm day).

Preheat the oven to 400°F. Bake until nicely browned and crisp on
both bottom and top, about 30 minutes. Eat while still a little warm.

CHERRY CLAFOUTIS

DON'T PIT THE CHERRIES, AS THEY ADD TO THE FLAVOR HERE.
This is an amazing yet simple dessert.

SERVES 6
all-purpose flour, *½ cup*
salt, *a pinch*
milk, *1 cup*
extra-large eggs, beaten, *2*
sugar, *¼ cup*
fresh sweet cherries, *1 pound*
unsalted butter, *1 tablespoon*

Preheat the oven to 400°F. Put the flour and salt in a bowl. Slowly pour in the milk and eggs, whisking to make a smooth batter, then stir in half of the sugar.

Put the cherries in a shallow 8-inch round baking dish. Add the butter and remaining sugar. Bake for 10 minutes. Pour the batter over the cherries and bake for 20 minutes longer.

AVIATION

I PREFER COCKTAILS TO BE MADE FOR ME IN A GLAMOROUS BAR...
But if you were going to make them yourself at home, this is what you'd do.
Maraschino is a fantastic bittersweet liqueur made from Marasca cherries.

MAKES 1
gin, *2 shots*
fresh lemon juice, *½ shot*
Maraschino, *½ shot*
violet syrup, *a few drops*
cherry, *1*
twist of lemon, *for garnish*

Shake all the liquids with ice, then strain into a martini glass. Drop in the cherry and finish with a twist of lemon.

Don't have too many even though they are delicious.

A KERALAN FEAST

M Y *favorite supper clubs are often those that feature food from India. The first of my Moveable Kitchen series was held on the top floor of a rowing club near my barge. This is, more or less, the menu I cooked. It was an attempt to recreate a fantastic meal I had at a temple near Kochi in Kerala. I love Keralan food, which is so very delicate and delightful.*

FRESH GINGER AND TAMARIND PICKLE

SERVES 6
tamarind block, *1 golfball-sized lump*
flavorless oil, *a splash*
mustard seeds, *1 teaspoon*
ground fenugreek seeds, *½ teaspoon*
fresh ginger, minced, *⅓ cup*
fresh, hot green chiles, minced, *2*
fresh curry leaves, *1 sprig*
Kashmiri chile powder, *1 teaspoon*
jaggery or brown sugar, *1 teaspoon*

In a small bowl, mash the tamarind with ½ cup boiling water. Let soak until soft, about 10 minutes, then push through a strainer into a bowl.

Heat the oil in a frying pan and crackle the mustard and fenugreek. When they are sputtering, add the ginger, chiles, and curry leaves. Fry for a few minutes, stirring occasionally. Add the tamarind liquid, chile powder, sugar, and salt to taste. Cook until reduced to a thick paste.

Check the balance and seasoning: the flavors should be zingy and strong, so add more tamarind, salt, or sugar if needed. Put the chutney into a little bowl and let cool.

POLLICHATTU

CHOOSE A HEAVY COCONUT, SO YOU KNOW IT IS FULL OF LIQUID. *Smash it, then prize out and peel the flesh to grate.*

SERVES 6

for the marinade
black pepper, *½ teaspoon*
ground turmeric, *¼ teaspoon*
lemon, *½*

for the pollichattu
cod or other white fish, *4 thick pieces, about 5 ounces each*
flavorless oil, *a splash*
mustard seeds, *1 heaping teaspoon*
dried, large red chiles, torn into pieces, *2*
scallions, minced, *3*
garlic cloves, green sprout removed, minced, *2*
fresh ginger, minced, *a thumb-sized piece*
fresh curry leaves, minced, *20*
fresh, hot green chiles, minced, *2*
cilantro leaves, minced, *2 tablespoons*
coconut, flesh grated (see page 73), *1*

Mix together the pepper, turmeric, and lemon juice, then rub this all over the pieces of fish. Set aside for about 30 minutes. Heat a small frying pan until very hot, then pour in sufficient oil to cover the bottom. Add the mustard seeds, then the dried chiles; now quickly throw in all the minced things before the spices burn. Cook briskly for a few minutes until some parts are a bit brown, then add the coconut and mix well to combine all the flavors. Add some salt.

Pat the fish dry, then cover it in the coconut mixture. Wrap in a banana leaf, securing the package with kitchen string, or in a sheet of foil. Grill over hot coals, or broil 4–6 inches from the heat source, for 6–8 minutes, depending on the thickness of the fish.

AVIAL

THIS VEGETABLE MIXTURE MAKES A GREAT DINNER ON ITS OWN. *Just add some pickle and a Chapati (see page 10). I like to include carrots, potatoes, and sometimes cauliflower. Green beans are nice, too. If you can find Keralan vegetable drumstick, do include it. The sour mango can be replaced by a squeeze of lime juice.*

SERVES 6 AS PART OF A FEAST,
OR 2 OR 3 ON ITS OWN
mixed vegetables, *1½ pounds*
garlic clove, green sprout removed, *1*
ground cumin, *a little pinch*
fresh ginger, chopped, *¾-inch piece*
fresh curry leaves, *20*
fresh coconut flesh, grated (see page 73), *1 heaping cup*
plain yogurt, *1 cup*
hot chile powder, *a pinch*
ground turmeric, *a pinch*
sour mango, chopped up small, *1-inch piece*
fresh, hot green chiles, slit in half, *3*

Cut the vegetables into pieces of a similar size—such as like a small cauliflower floret. If you have found drumstick, scrape it to remove some of the dark green, then cut it into 4-inch lengths.

Crush the garlic with the cumin and a little salt. Add the ginger and curry leaves and continue to crush until you have a roughish paste. Mash in the coconut and then the yogurt.

Layer the vegetables in a saucepan, starting with potato (if using) and ending with the type that takes the least time to cook. Add 1 cup water, some salt, the chile powder, and turmeric. Cover and cook until the potato is soft. If there is any liquid left, remove the lid and continue to cook until almost all is evaporated.

Add the coconut mixture, sour mango, and slit chiles and mix; don't worry if the vegetables break up. Taste for salt. Let the avial sit for a while before you eat it. Don't worry too much about the temperature of the dish—it's nice just warmish.

CARDAMOM MILK

WHEN BUYING CARDAMOM, CHOOSE PODS THAT ARE VIVID GREEN.
Old or second-grade cardamom has a dusty green color.

SERVES 6
whole milk, *1 quart*
cardamom pods, *a large handful*
sugar, *to taste*
slivered almonds, *½ cup*
mangoes, preferably Alphonso, *3*
saffron strands, *a few*

Bring the milk just to a boil with the cardamom. Once it has boiled,
pour into a clean, heavy-based pan and boil, gently and regularly
stirring, until reduced by half. It is important not to burn the milk,
because this will ruin your dessert. Stir in sugar to taste—remember
that it will taste less sweet when cool. Refrigerate until completely
cold, then stir in the almonds. When you are ready to eat, and you have
prepared your mangoes (see page 71), put a few strands of saffron into
each glass and pour in some of the cool milk. Eat the mango alongside.

During the summer, many ingredients are at their peak and require far less cooking. In fact, summer meals are often more about careful shopping and delicate seasoning than anything complicated, or that involves time-consuming preparation. Sometimes it's simply a case of assembling the very best things you can find and combining them sensitively. We had a great July birthday lunch that was entirely made up of such an assemblage (see page 102).

Okra is particularly good in the summer. The fingers are smaller, the seeds are less developed, and the pods tend to be less slimy (not that I mind slimy). If you're yet to be convinced, try some of the recipes in this chapter. You might be surprised (see page 108).

While everything in the garden is so plentiful, it's a good time of year to consider the damage we have done to the environment we can't see. The world's fish stocks are of particular concern (see page 100). We can all help, by being curious about what we buy and eat, and getting to know our fish merchants.

MYSTIC TUNA

Tuna is an incredible fish, majestic and sought-after for a good reason. I think it is at its best raw. My choice for cooking is the cheek, or the bit from the top of the head.

Seeing the tuna auction at Tsukiji Shijo (the massive fish market in Tokyo) is an incredible experience. In this enormous cathedral of a warehouse, the fish lie on the floor like gleaming torpedoes. Men in white rubber boots inspect them with little ice picks, shining torches through morsels of flesh to tell the quality, looking for the rich fat so loved by the Japanese, checking for any signs of parasites or disease before the auction begins, and deciding what price to pay.

The beginning of the auction is announced by a man standing on a box. He rings a bell and starts to chant. Another man interrupts, then another, and another, until a sticker is fixed onto the fish and it is hauled away. It is like a sacred ritual.

After the auction the fish is taken to the outer market, to a respected tuna wholesaler, where the beast is expertly cut using a knife as long as the man who wields it. The beautiful knives are made in one of the ancient samurai-swordmaking houses. Each cut is precise and fast. A couple of apprentices help, removing each of the four enormous fillets with a wooden board for the master to divide into the various cuts: *maguro* (lean), *chutoro* (medium fatty), and, the most prized, *otoro*.

Without doubt, the Japanese love tuna more than any other people in the world. The fish is such an important part of their culinary culture that it is surprising they don't look after their tuna stocks and protect them.

The truth is that tuna, particularly bluefin, is endangered. Really endangered. It has been over-fished to such an extent that it is very likely my children will never taste real *otoro*. Depleted fish stocks are a worldwide issue, and one that—as with everything from human rights to global warming—it seems impossible for us to sort out. We try to regulate, but rarely can enforce.

There has been some success: by selling quotas of fish to fishermen, some administrations have given them a vested interest in maintaining fish stocks. It has meant that fewer fish are caught and those that are fetch a higher price.

What is really needed is commitment and you can help. When buying always ask about your fish: find out if it was pole-and-line-caught (much less damaging) or caught by a trawler (disastrous for the sea bed), and if it has flown across the world or come from local waters. Fish-farming practices need to improve, too: at the moment too many farms produce flabby fish fed on smaller fish caught destructively by trawler. Generally, for both taste and eco-footprint, carefully-caught wild fish is the best option.

My hope is that in the future we will be able to look after the ocean, farming what we cannot catch, catching what we can without taking more than we should, and preserving the taste of *otoro* for the next generations.

A BIRTHDAY CELEBRATION HELD ON BOARD

I **WAS** *very happy to cook this meal for an old friend. I love to make a table of food for everyone to help themselves. When all these dishes were on separate plates, they stood out in their own simple way. On reflection I realized that I had made a kind of deconstructed Niçoise salad, needing only a plate of boiled new potatoes with parsley and oil to complete the elements.*

EGGS AND OLIVES

USE GOOD BLACK OLIVES, THE TYPE FROM THE SOUTH OF FRANCE.

SERVES 10
thyme leaves, *1 teaspoon*
garlic clove, green sprout removed, *½*
brandy, *a splash*
olive oil
black olives, *½ cup*
capers, *1 teaspoon*
yellow celery leaves, *a few*
eggs, hard-cooked (see page 59), *10*

Crush the thyme and garlic together with a little salt in a mortar and pestle. Add the brandy and some olive oil, to produce the consistency of a dressing. Chop the olives, capers, and celery leaves together. Put these in a bowl and stir in the thyme mixture. Sprinkle with black pepper and taste. When you are ready to eat, peel the eggs, cut them in half, and top with bits of the olivey stuff.

GREEN BEANS

I LIKE TO USE THE THIN GREEN BEANS KNOWN AS HARICOTS VERTS. *Any green beans will work, however. I've heard that Kenya grows most of the green beans sold in the world. I've never been there, but imagine it must be a land full of green beans. Sometimes I add a few salted anchovy fillets to this dish just before the beans. It's wonderful.*

SERVES 10
green beans, hard tops removed, *1 pound*
garlic cloves, green sprout removed, sliced thinly, *2*
olive oil, *a splash*
parsley, chopped, *a small handful*

Bring a large pot of salty water to a boil. Tip in the green beans and boil for a few minutes until just tender. Drain.

Fry the garlic in the oil until it is just about to turn a little brown. Add the parsley and then the green beans. Season and cook together for a few minutes until the flavors are combined.

LARGE RIDGED TOMATOES, ROASTED

Preheat the oven to 350°F. Choose 4 big, well-flavored tomatoes. Slice them thickly, splash with olive oil, and season well with salt and pepper. Sprinkle with both fresh and dried oregano. Roast until soft but still in shape, about 20 minutes. Put them on a plate and eat warm or cold.

CONFIT TUNA

WHEN BUYING YOUR TUNA FOR THIS, BE AN INQUIRING SHOPPER. *Look for tuna certified as sustainable to the standard of the Marine Steward-ship Council (MSC). Use the loin or belly and cut the fish into rough cubes.*

SERVES 10
tuna, *10 pieces, about 5 ounces each*
twigs of hard herbs, such as rosemary, wild fennel, myrtle, and thyme, *a few*
dried, small hot chiles, *2*
parsley stalks, *a few*
black peppercorns, *a few*
fennel seeds, *1 teaspoon*
coriander seeds, *a few*
medium-good olive oil, *about 4 cups*

Season the tuna very well with salt and set aside while you gather the other ingredients that will be used to flavor the oil. Put the tuna and all the herb twigs in a pan that is big enough so that the pieces of fish are not squashed together, and that will allow the tuna to be submerged in oil without wasting too much.

Add all the remaining ingredients to the pan and cover with oil. Warm over medium-low heat until the oil is just too hot to dip in your finger (about 140°F if you have a thermometer). Remove from the heat and transfer to a cold bowl. Let the fish cool in the oil.

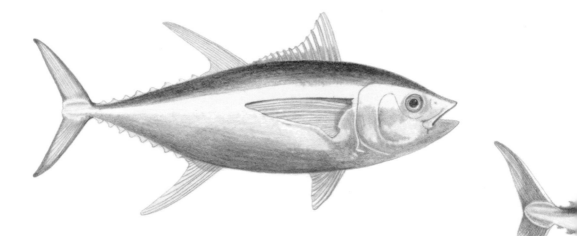

CHOCOLATE, HAZELNUT, BRANDY, AND ESPRESSO CAKE

I LOVE HAVING SO MANY OF MY FAVORITE THINGS IN ONE RECIPE. *This is a great cake that I could eat at any time of day.*

SERVES 10–12

good unsalted butter, plus more for the pan, *1⅓ cups*
eggs, *6*
sugar, *1¼ cups*
really good bittersweet chocolate, *14 ounces*
whole blanched, roasted hazelnuts, *2 heaping cups*
unsweetened cocoa powder, *1 heaping tablespoon*
espresso or very black coffee, *⅔ cup*
brandy, *½ cup*

Preheat the oven to 325°F. Butter an 8-inch springform cake pan, then line with parchment paper.

Beat the eggs with the sugar for about 10 minutes; the mixture should triple in volume.

Melt the chocolate and butter together in a bowl set over a pan of simmering water (make sure the base of the bowl does not touch the water). Grind the hazelnuts and cocoa together medium-fine; don't grind too long or they will turn oily.

Add the coffee and brandy to the chocolate, then mix this concoction into the eggs. Gently mix in the hazelnuts. Pour into the pan. Bake until dry on the top and not too wobbly beneath, about 40 minutes.

A RAINY EVENING: SUPPER FOR TWO

THE *heavy rain in summer can sometimes feel very like a monsoon all of our own. I love the sound of it hammering on the roof of the barge and the way it falls onto the river and blurs the sight of the bridge. On a night like this it is, of course, best to stay at home and eat tamarind rice watching the rain. It's a great recipe because, if you have a well-stocked spice cupboard, you don't have to go to the market. Don't worry if you don't have all the ingredients: apart from the rice and tamarind I seem to change it most times I cook it. I learned to make this on an equally rainy day on a tea plantation in Sri Lanka. It was a particularly beautiful place, as our picker's cottage was at the top of the valley, looking out over the tea plants and the papaya trees. A local cook gathered gota kola leaves, shredded them very finely, and added them at the end of the recipe. If you want to add greens to your rice, any dryish bitter leaves would work—turnip or beet greens would be good. Make this when you need a little comfort.*

TAMARIND RICE

I LIKE A BIT OF HOME-GROWN SLICED CUCUMBER AND TOMATO *on the side with this dish.*

SERVES 2
short-grain Thai rice, *½ cup*
tamarind block, *a piece the size of a lemon*
flavorless oil, *1 tablespoon*
mustard seeds, *½ teaspoon*
white urud dhal (lentil), optional, *½ teaspoon*
fresh, hot green chiles, *2*
dried, hot red chile, *1*
small red onion, minced, *1*
fresh curry leaves, *a few*
ground fenugreek, *½ teaspoon*
ground turmeric, *¼ teaspoon*
ground cumin, *a pinch*
cashew nuts, *a handful*

Rinse the rice well, then simmer it in 1 cup salted water on a medium heat for 5 minutes (it will be half-cooked). Remove from the heat and drain, then return to the warm pan. Cover with the lid and set aside. Soak the tamarind in 1 cup boiling water; when it has cooled enough to put your fingers in the water, do so and mush the tamarind into the water to make a flavorful juice.

Warm another pan and pour in the oil. Add the mustard seeds and dhal, if using. When they crackle, add the two types of chile. Then add the onion and the curry leaves. Add the rest of the spices. Once the onion has lost its raw smell, add the nuts. Cook for a few more minutes, stirring, until the flavor of the spices is released and the onion is soft.

Strain the tamarind liquid into the pan. Boil to reduce, stirring, until quite thick; be careful not to burn it. Separate the grains of rice with a fork, then add the rice to the pan and mix just a little. It's nice when some of the rice is more flavored than other parts.

SUMMER OKRA

Okra is a mysterious vegetable. For a long time I tried to cook it in a way that made it not-slimy. Then I realized that it's not all that slimy, and also that a little slime never did anyone any harm. In July, at the Dock Kitchen, there is okra on the menu most days. It is at its best in the summer, when Middle Eastern and Greek varieties are at their peak. Try to choose small okra that won't have developed big seeds.

POTATOES WITH OKRA NAXOS-STYLE

THIS IS A RECIPE I FOUND IN PATIENCE GRAY'S EXCELLENT BOOK, *Honey from a Weed*.

SERVES 4
red onions, thinly sliced, *2*
olive oil, *½ cup*
garlic cloves, green sprout removed, sliced, *6*
semi-waxy potatoes, *10–12 ounces*
okra, *10–12 ounces*
plum tomato, torn into pieces, *1*
cilantro, chopped, *½ bunch*

Fry the onions in the oil over low heat. After a few minutes, add the garlic. Meanwhile, peel the potatoes and cut into pieces 1½ inches long. Boil them in salty water until just cooked. When the onion is soft and sweet, add the okra and tomato. Cook until the okra is soft, about 10 minutes, then add the potatoes. Season well and add the cilantro. Cook together for a few minutes; don't worry if it all breaks up a bit.

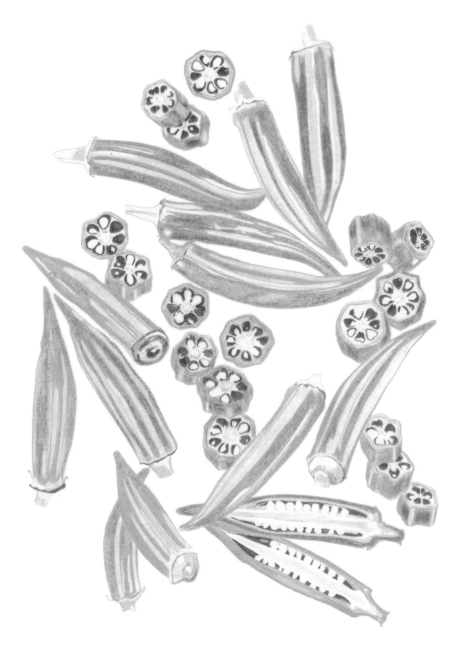

OKRA DEEP-FRIED IN GRAM FLOUR WITH MUSTARD SEEDS, CHILES, AND CURRY LEAVES (BHINDI BHAJI)

THIS IS A GREAT WAY TO START A MEAL, AND IS VERY ADAPTABLE. *Sometimes cauliflower, shrimp, or even potatoes have joined the okra in its batter. Bhajis a bit like this are eaten all over India. You can vary their contents with the season, using practically anything you fancy.*

SERVES 6

mustard seeds, *1 teaspoon*
fennel seeds, *¾ teaspoon*
cumin seeds, *¾ teaspoon*
okra, *7 ounces*
besan or gram flour (chickpea flour), *1¾ cups*
salt, *1 teaspoon*
sunflower oil, *for deep-frying*
fresh curry leaves, *25*
cilantro sprigs, leaves minced, *a few*
fresh, hot green chiles, minced, *2–6*
plain yogurt (optional), *½ cup*

Toast each of the seeds separately in a medium-hot dry pan: let them crackle for a few seconds, then remove to a plate before they burn and become bitter. Slice the okra into ½-inch pieces, removing the stalks.

Sift the besan into a bowl and add the salt. Whisk in ⅔ cup water. Keep whisking until you have a thick, lumpfree paste. Add the spices and slowly whisk in ½–⅔ cup more water to make a reasonably thick batter. Heat about 2 inches of oil in a pan at least 6 inches deep.

Add the sliced okra, curry leaves, cilantro, and chiles to the batter. When the oil is very hot, but not smoking (350°F if you are using a thermometer), drizzle in the batter to make long drops of fried okra. Drizzle slowly to avoid creating big, doughy bhajis. Deep-fry until crisp and light brown. Serve with a little yogurt, or just salt.

OKRA WITH TOMATOES

THIS IS THE WONDERFUL WAY THEY COOK OKRA IN NORTH INDIA.
It is quite amazing with a Chapati (see page 10).

SERVES 4
flavorless oil
ground cumin, *a pinch*
red onions, sliced thinly into half-moons, *3*
fresh ginger, minced, *¾-inch piece*
garlic cloves, green sprout removed, chipped, *2*
ground coriander, *1 tablespoon*
ground turmeric, *a pinch*
mild chile powder, *¾ teaspoon*
okra, tops cut off, *1 pound*
plum tomatoes, quartered, *2*

Heat a wide pan and pour in enough oil to cover the bottom well.
Add the cumin. When it crackles, add the onions, ginger, and garlic,
and reduce the heat. Add the rest of the spices and season well. Cook,
stirring occasionally, until the onion has broken down and is soft, about
15 minutes.

Add the okra and tomatoes to the pan and continue to cook on
low heat, breaking up the tomato, until the okra is soft but hasn't
completely fallen apart. This will take about 15 minutes, depending
on the size of the okra.

LAMB, OKRA, AND TOMATO TASHREEB

TASHREEB IS A COMMON IRAQI DISH, THOUGH IT IS UNUSUAL TO US. *The word comes from sharaab, "to drink," referring to the way the pita bread under the stew soaks up the liquid.*

SERVES 6
ground allspice, *1 tablespoon*
ground coriander, *1 teaspoon*
unsmoked paprika or mild chile powder, *1 teaspoon*
small lamb shoulder on the bone, *1*
olive oil
garlic cloves, peeled but left whole, *6*
plum tomatoes, roughly chopped, *15*
dried lime, left whole, *1*
pomegranate molasses (if you have some), *2 tablespoons*
pita breads, *6*
small okra, *1 pound*

Rub the spices onto the lamb and season well with salt and pepper. Heat a wide pan that will accommodate the whole shoulder with a bit of space to move it. Fry the lamb gently in some olive oil until well browned. Be careful not to burn the spices. Throw in the garlic, then add the tomatoes and dried lime.

Add enough water almost to cover the lamb and pour in the pomegranate molasses, if using. Cover and cook gently (with the water just about bubbling) until the lamb is tender, about 2 hours.

Preheat the oven to 350°F. Put the pita bread into the oven to dry out until it is hard.

Add the okra to the lamb and continue simmering until the okra is tender. Tear the lamb from the bone and put it in a large, shallow serving bowl with the pita bread. Pour the okra and cooking liquid over.

DEEP-FRIED OKRA MIXED WITH YOGURT AND POMEGRANATE

I FOUND THIS DISH WHEN I WORKED AT MORO IN LONDON.
It's particularly good with roast chicken.

SERVES 4
okra, *8 ounces*
sunflower oil, *for deep-frying*
thick yogurt, *½ cup*
mint and cilantro, *a few leaves*
pomegranate seeds, *from ½ fruit*

Cut the okra into ½-inch rounds, discarding the hard stalk.

Heat about 2 inches of oil in a deep pan. Deep-fry the okra, in batches, until starting to brown. Remove with a slotted spoon and drain off the excess oil on paper towels. Mix the fried okra with the yogurt, whole herb leaves, and pomegranate, then season with salt and pepper.

August is a month of bounty on the vegetable plot. Your hard
work is finally being rewarded by more green beans (see page 116),
tomatoes, corn, and chiles than you can eat. There is very little
actual work to do, other than harvest. So for me this is the perfect
time for slowing down and sitting on the deck of my boat, enjoying
the warm days and long, warm evenings.

At this time of year, lunch is often a chunk of soda bread (see page
126), some sliced tomatoes, and a good Cheddar, evoking memories
of vacations in my dad's village in Ireland.

DELICIOUS FINE GREEN BEANS

Green beans are a handy thing to have around, with many possibilities.

They are wonderful…

…blanched, then fried with garlic and parsley
…eaten raw as a snack, just pulled off the plant while weeding at the plot
…in an avial (see page 96)
…blanched, then fried with garlic, chile, and a couple of anchovy fillets

PARMIGIANI

THIS RELIES ON PARMESAN, FRESH BEANS, GOOD OIL, AND LEMONS. *I love the large-leafed arugula from Middle-Eastern markets. It often looks a bit floppy, but is easily revived by soaking in a sink of cold water.*

SERVES 4
large-leafed arugula, *3 bunches*
green beans, tops cut off, *7 ounces*
Parmesan, freshly grated, *¾ cup*
good olive oil
juicy lemon, *1*

Wash and dry the arugula. Boil the beans in a big pan of salted water until soft, then drain well. Mix the cheese with a couple of generous slugs of olive oil, most of the lemon juice, and lots of black pepper. Add the warm beans and mix. Check the seasoning. Dress the arugula with a little oil and a squeeze of lemon, then place the warm beans on top.

SZECHUAN WITH LITTLE BITS OF PORK

EAT WITH A BOWL OF RICE, OR ADD FRIED TOFU AND GRILLED FISH. *In Szechuan, they use yard-long beans for this dish. If you can find these in Asian markets, substitute them for the green beans here.*

SERVES 4 – 6
green beans, tops cut off, *8 ounces*
garlic clove, green sprout removed, *1*
anise seeds, *1 teaspoon*
crushed dried chile, *1 teaspoon*
Szechuan pepper, *½ teaspoon*
ground pork, *3 ounces*
flavorless oil, *a splash*
fresh ginger, grated, *2-inch piece*
rice wine vinegar, *a splash*

Chop the beans up a bit. Crush the garlic in a mortar; add the spices and crush until you have a paste. Mix this well with the pork. Roll the pork into little bits about the size of a marble.

Heat a large pan or wok and pour in the oil. Put in the little bits of pork and fry them, stirring. When they start to crisp a bit, throw in the beans and ginger. Fry until the beans start to look cooked. Add the vinegar, reduce the heat, and cook until the beans are soft.

A LIGURIAN SUPPER FOR SOME FRIENDS, WHO WOULD ALL PREFER TO BE ON VACATION BUT HAVE INSTEAD TO WORK

I LOVE *to start a meal like this with a plate of fish. Sometimes I prepare boiled octopus, mixed with potatoes, chopped celery, olive oil, and parsley, or roast a whole fish and let it cool. Recently I have been making sardines escabeche. You butterfly the sardines and fry them skin side down, being careful not to cook them all the way through, then lay them out flat and pour a mixture of confit garlic, red wine vinegar, bay leaves, salt, and hot paprika over them.*

This Ligurian feast begins with a plate of clams, chickpeas, and marinated anchovies. It's a good combination. If you can't find fresh anchovies, you can treat other small silver fish in the same way. If the fish are bigger than anchovies, leave them in the vinegar and lemon until they look cooked before you add the oil. I follow the fish with pasta dressed with pesto and end with fruit in wine. The menu is one of my favorite meals for this time of year. All of the recipes serve 10.

MARINATED FRESH ANCHOVIES

YOU CAN OFTEN FIND FRESH ANCHOVIES IN ETHNIC MARKETS.
When you take the time to fillet and marinate them, the result is very good.
Pacific anchovies have a stronger flavor than their Mediterranean cousins, but
both are excellent fresh. I often vary the seasonings for this recipe—sometimes
using lemon, sometimes vinegar, and adding flavorings such as oregano, parsley,
marjoram, chile, and fennel leaves.

> fresh anchovies, *2¼ pounds*
> juicy lemons, *4*
> crushed dried chile, *to taste*
> parsley, chopped, *a small handful*
> grated lemon zest, *from 2 of the lemons*
> fennel seeds, ground, *1 teaspoon*
> delicate olive oil, *1 cup*

Fillet the anchovies by pulling the fillets from the bones—a bit like
peeling a banana. Scrape the guts from the flesh a little, but don't rinse
the fillets. Lay them in a bowl. Squeeze the lemon juice over them,
season with salt, and toss them around a bit so the lemon is coating all
of them. Set aside so the lemon juice can "cook" the fish. After an hour,
check the fish; when ready they should be gray in color, not pink.
Remove them from the juice and arrange silver-side up on a flat dish.
When you have made one layer, sprinkle the various seasonings over
them in any quantity that looks nice (but be careful not to make them
too spicy). Repeat the process until all your anchovies are used up, then
pour the olive oil over the top.

CHICKPEAS AND WILD OREGANO

A VERY CHEAP AND SEEMINGLY UNEXCITING DISH, THIS IS AMAZING. *It sits perfectly as a subtle complement to most Italian-inspired feasts. You must use really good dried wild oregano, preferably from Italy or Greece. As this is such a simple dish, poor-quality or old dried herbs have nowhere to hide—especially not at the back of a cupboard in your kitchen. Throw them out.*

dried large chickpeas, *1½ cups*
celery rib, roughly chopped, *1*
tomato, torn into big pieces, *1*
garlic cloves, peeled, *4*
good fresh, sweet olive oil, *a generous dose*
good dried, wild oregano, *a few pinches*

Soak the chickpeas overnight, then rinse them thoroughly in the morning, removing any bits of stalk or loose skin that float to the top of the water. Cover them with fresh water and boil them gently with the celery, tomato, and whole garlic cloves. Do not add salt, which would make the skins tough. Cook until the chickpeas are almost completely soft. Sometimes this takes 40 minutes; at other times it can take as long as 2 hours. Season with salt, then set aside.

When you are soon to eat, warm the chickpeas, then drain them of most of their liquid. Discard the celery, garlic, and tomato; they have served their purpose.

Put the chickpeas on a big platter, then dose liberally with olive oil and sprinkle with dried oregano.

A BIG PLATE OF CLAMS

SPAGHETTI IS AN EXCELLENT ADDITION TO MAKE THIS A MEAL.
Sometimes I add curry leaves and coconut (see page 177). At other times of year you could try Chardonnay and porcini, some pieces of dry bread, and olive oil.

cheap extra-virgin olive oil
garlic cloves, green sprout removed, minced, *4*
dried, small, hot chiles, crushed, *2*
fresh littleneck clams, cleaned, *1½ pounds*
large, ripe tomatoes, chopped up a bit, *4*
parsley, chopped, *a small handful*
white wine, *a splash*

Choose a wide pan that will accommodate all the clams in not too deep a layer (if you would have to pile them up high in your widest pan, steam them in a few batches instead, or they will cook unevenly). Heat the pan and pour in enough olive oil to coat the bottom well. Make sure all the ingredients are on hand, because you have to move fast.

Quickly throw in the garlic, followed by the chile. Before the garlic or chile burn, throw in the clams, tomatoes, parsley, and wine. Put the lid on the pan and cook on high heat until all the clams are open. This will only take a few minutes. Discard any that remain stubbornly shut and warn your diners to do the same.

TROFIE PESTO

TROFIE IS A PASTA SHAPE THAT IS GOOD EITHER FRESH OR DRIED.
*Fresh lasagnette or fusilli would make excellent substitutes. It's important to
use a delicate oil, not a strong Tuscan example. A buttery oil from Liguria or
the south of Italy would be perfect. When I see enormous bunches of young,
soft basil in the market, I can't help but make pesto. Using a blender will give
you a brighter, smoother pesto, but I prefer to make it by hand with a mortar
and pestle. I think that grinding the basil with the garlic and salt gives a far
superior flavor.*

> garlic clove, green sprout removed, *1*
> big bunches of basil, leaves picked off the stems,
>   carefully washed and dried, *2*
> good-quality pine nuts, *a small handful*
> aged pecorino or Parmesan, or a bit of both, grated, *a big handful*
> ricotta, 1 *tablespoon*, or milk, *a splash*
> olive oil, *½ cup*
> trofie or other pasta, 1¾ *pounds*

In a large mortar, grind the garlic with a pinch of sea salt. Add as
much basil as you can and grind it, using a circular motion. As the basil
starts to break down, add more, until all of it is incorporated into a
green, headily scented paste. Add the pine nuts and grind some more
(it doesn't matter if you have a few chunkier pieces), then grind in
the cheese. Add the ricotta or milk, then stir in enough oil to make a
smooth, green, aromatic pesto. Check the seasonings.

Cook your pasta of choice al dente. Drain, reserving a little of the
pasta cooking water. Dress the pasta with the pesto, adding enough
of the pasta water to create a smooth, luxurious dish. Traditionally, in
Liguria, you get a piece or two of boiled potato and some green beans
mixed in with the pasta. It sounds a little strange but is really delicious.

PEACHES AND CHERRIES IN RED WINE

THIS IS A VERY SIMPLE, YET EXCEEDINGLY ELEGANT END TO A MEAL. *Make sure your fruits are excellent examples at their peak of flavor.*

> Valpolicella or other light red wine, *1 bottle*
> large black cherries, *a big plate*
> delicious ripe, flat peaches, *a big plate*

Pour all of your guests half a glass of wine and encourage them to tear cherries and peaches into the glass, then leave it for half an hour. (It's important to ensure that everyone has another drink readily on hand, otherwise temptation takes over and the wine is drunk before the fruit has had enough time to sit in it.)

When half an hour is up, or you and your guests can wait no longer, eat the fruit and drink the wine.

Follow with a glass of grappa.

SALT

Salt is an essential. I often think of Gandhi leading a march across India to boil water on the shores to make salt, thus avoiding the British salt tax.

Putting enough salt in your food is basic. Before you can begin to think about more complex seasonings, you need to have added enough salt to be able to taste the food properly. Salt makes food taste more of itself. It turns up the volume.

There is a right amount of salt that any one dish needs, so you must taste repeatedly and carefully. Add salt as near to the start of cooking as possible (with the exception of dried beans or watery vegetables that you intend to fry, because the salt pulls out the liquid). This way you will need less salt and your supper will be more thoroughly seasoned than if you add salt at the end. When boiling pasta or vegetables, the water should be almost as salty as the sea.

Salt is an excellent preservative, too. I have salted everything from plums to pig's ears, always with interesting results.

All salt is basically NaCl, sodium chloride. The sodium is the important salty bit, and the many different types of salt—whether it be kosher salt or flaked sea salt, from Bolivia or the Carmargue in France—contain the same amount. What makes the difference is the texture or, for the cook, the way it feels in the hand. Cooks prefer to season with a coarse salt that you can feel easily—it helps you get to know intuitively how much you need. Trying to season with fine salt is trickier, because you just can't feel it in the same way. The exception, of course, is baking, where fine salt is the one to use.

I hate cooking without good salt.

SALTED HAZELNUT ICE CREAM

THIS IS A GREAT ICE CREAM THAT I AM ALWAYS VERY HAPPY TO EAT. *I love the way the salt in the caramel makes it deliciously savory. As always with ice cream, it is important to use good cream, milk, and eggs.*

SERVES 6
milk, *1 cup*
heavy cream, *1 cup*
vanilla bean, *1*
hazelnuts, blanched, *1½ cups*
butter, *1 teaspoon*
Demerara sugar, *⅓ cup*
Maldon salt, *a sprinkle*
egg yolks, *5*
granulated sugar, *¼ cup*

Preheat the oven to 350°F. Put the milk and cream in a heavy-based saucepan. Split the vanilla bean lengthwise and scrape out the seeds. Add both seeds and pod to the milk. Place over low heat.

Combine the nuts, butter, Demerara sugar, and salt in a baking pan and toast in the oven until the sugar has melted and the nuts are light brown, about 5 minutes. Watch carefully so the nuts don't burn. Let cool. Whisk the egg yolks with the granulated sugar.

Increase the heat under the milk and, just before it boils, pour it onto the egg yolks, whisking all the time. Pour the mixture back into the pan and return to low heat. Stir until the custard coats the back of a wooden spoon. Be careful not to let it get too hot, otherwise the egg will start to scramble and the custard will be lumpy. You can check with your finger occasionally: the custard should not be too hot to hold your finger in it. When the custard has thickened, let cool, stirring occasionally, then refrigerate to chill.

Grind the cooled nuts. Mix them into the custard, then churn in an ice cream machine until frozen.

MY DAD'S SODA BREAD

THE *smell of soda bread baking always takes me back to the little cottage we used to have in the 1950s in the south of Ireland. It was in the village my dad is from, and he taught me how to make soda bread. Making it with him is one of my earliest memories. Soda bread is so quick and easy. Sometimes I make it in the afternoon and eat it as soon as it is cool enough, with butter and jam, or with a good sharp cheese.*

MAKES 1 LOAF
all-purpose flour, sifted, *3 cups*
salt, *1 teaspoon*
baking soda, *1 teaspoon*
buttermilk, *1¾ cups*

Preheat the oven to 425°F. Put the flour, salt, and soda into a big bowl. Make a well in the center of the flour and pour in the buttermilk. Mix with your hand: open your fingers into a claw shape and quickly bring the dough together. Turn it out onto a well-floured surface and shape into a round about 4 inches thick. Flour a baking sheet and set your loaf on it. Score a large cross about 1½ inches deep on top.

Bake until browned, about 10 minutes, then reduce the oven temperature to 350°F and continue baking until the bread sounds hollow when you tap the base, about 30 minutes longer. Let the loaf cool on a wire rack before you break it up to eat.

BROWN SODA BREAD

Soda bread is different from other breads in that it mustn't be worked too much. So don't knead it. And use a flour that will make a good-tasting bread.

MAKES 1 LOAF
whole wheat flour, *4 cups*
all-purpose flour, *⅔ cup*
salt, *1 teaspoon*
baking soda, *1 teaspoon*
egg, *1*
oil, *1 tablespoon*
molasses, *1 teaspoon*
buttermilk, *2 cups*

Preheat the oven to 425°F. Sift the dry ingredients into a big bowl (and shake in the bran from the whole wheat flour left behind in the sifter). Make a well in the center and add all the remaining ingredients. Mix quickly and confidently, with your hand in a claw shape. Turn the dough out onto a well-floured surface and shape it into a round, using a slow turning action. Push the bread down to make a loaf about 4 inches thick. Cut a cross all the way across the bread about 1½ inches deep.

Bake until brown, 10–15 minutes, then reduce the oven temperature to 350°F and continue baking until the loaf sounds hollow when you tap the base, about 30 minutes longer.

September is the crossover month. You still have delicious end-of-summer tomatoes—even if you have to find something to do with those that remain stubbornly green (see page 141)—while you are also looking toward the arrival of the first squashes and wild mushrooms of the fall.

It was during a sunny week at the end of September that I opened the Dock Kitchen, and was quickly overwhelmed by people buying our madeleines. We made thousands of these little cakes. Somehow, it didn't put me off them, and it was during this busy time that the variations on the excellent original recipe arose (see page 132)—perhaps because it's nicer if the five hundredth madeleine tastes a little different from the tenth.

REMEMBERING A WEEKEND IN PORTUGAL

THE *Portuguese, it is said, have a bacalhau dish for every day of the year. I can believe it. Here's my favorite, which is delicious with a vinegary tomato salad on the side. It's easier to use the less dry, thinner salt cod when cooking it to eat as a piece. Be inquisitive about the source of your fish, and discuss its sustainability with your fish merchant.*

SALT COD WITH CHICKPEAS

SERVES 4

salt cod, *4 pieces, about 4 ounces each*
dried chickpeas, *1¼ cups,* or canned chickpeas, rinsed, *2 14-ounce cans*
garlic cloves, green sprout removed, thinly sliced, *4*
thyme sprigs, *a few*
parsley stalks, *a few*
black peppercorns, *a few*
carrots, peeled and cut lengthwise, *4*
eggs, *4*
parsley leaves, chopped, *a handful*
olive oil, *for serving*
lemons, *2*

Put the cod in a large container and place under slowly running water for an hour. Then refrigerate for at least 48 hours, changing the water a couple of times. Taste some fish (raw); it shouldn't be overly salty.

Soak and cook the dried chickpeas (see page 120), then season.

Put the drained cod in a wide pan with the garlic, thyme, parsley stalks, peppercorns, and carrots. Cover with water and cook over low heat, covered, until the cod flakes easily. Meanwhile, hard-cook and peel the eggs (see page 59); warm the chickpeas and drain.

Now assemble the plates. Each person needs a piece of cod, a carrot, some chickpeas, and an egg. Sprinkle with parsley—plus a little chopped onion to be authentic (I hate raw onion). Pour a generous amount of olive oil over each plate and put a wedge of lemon on the side.

TOMATO, BREAD, AND MUSSEL SOUP

THIS IS INSPIRED BY A BOWL OF SOUP I HAD IN THE TOWN OF BELEM. *It is the home of a beautiful cathedral and, more importantly, also of the world famous* pasteis de natas *(custard tarts).*

SERVES 6
plum tomatoes, *25*
good olive oil, *for frying and serving*
garlic cloves, green sprout removed, thinly sliced, *4*
hot smoked paprika, *¼ teaspoon*
fresh oregano, *a few sprigs*
good dry bread, *8 ounces*
rope-grown mussels, cleaned, *1 pound*
white wine, *a splash*

Peel the tomatoes: blanch in boiling water for 10 seconds, then refresh in cold water and pull off the skin. Squeeze the tomatoes and cut out the core.

Heat a wide, heavy-bottomed pan, pour in a little olive oil, and fry most of the garlic. When it starts to color and the slices stick together, add the paprika and oregano, then the tomatoes. Reduce the heat, cover, and let cook until thickened, about 1 hour, breaking up the tomatoes a bit every now and then with a wooden spoon.

Meanwhile, tear up the bread and put it into a low oven to dry out for a few minutes. Put the bread on top of the cooked tomato and moisten it with a little oil.

Heat another wide pan and fry the remaining garlic. Add the mussels and white wine, cover, and steam until the mussels open.

Break up the bread into the tomato, loosening the mixture with a little water if needed to make a thick, lumpy soup. Tip the mussels into a colander or strainer lined with cheesecloth and strain the juice into the tomato soup. Stir well. Serve each bowl of thick soup with a bit of olive oil and some mussels on top.

MADELEINES ST. JOHN-STYLE

THIS IS BASED ON AN EXCELLENT RECIPE FROM FERGUS HENDERSON. *He browns the butter and doesn't add orange flower water (they are great made that way, too). I cannot work out what the variable is that gives madeleines a dimple on the top; sometimes you get it and sometimes you don't. You will need a special madeleine pan to make these shell-shaped cakes.*

MAKES ABOUT 24
unsalted butter, plus more for the pan, *½ cup (1 stick) + 1 tablespoon*
good floral honey, *2 tablespoons*
orange flower water, *1 tablespoon*
extra-large eggs, *3*
light brown sugar, *1 heaping tablespoon*
granulated sugar, *½ cup + 1 tablespoon*
self-rising flour, plus more for the pan, *1 cup*

Melt the butter with the honey, then pour in the orange flower water and let cool. Beat the eggs and sugars together in an electric mixer until really fluffy, about 10 minutes. Fold in the flour, followed by the butter and honey mixture. Pour the batter into a container and let rest for at least 3 hours in the refrigerator (sometimes I leave it overnight).

Preheat the oven to 375°F. Butter a madeleine pan, then dust it with flour and tap out the excess. Spoon the batter into the molds, filling them two-thirds full. Bake until golden brown and firm to the touch, about 10 minutes.

BALANCING ACIDITY

Balance is important. I love my cooking to have just enough acidity to make it really zing. Lemon and vinegar generally provide this necessary sharpness in Western cooking, while Asian and Middle-Eastern cooks have all kinds of amazing ways to make their food suitably tangy, from tamarind and cocum, to mango powder and sumac. All cultures appreciate the importance of acidity to balance the flavors in food.

Try to think about this when you are cooking. Sometimes, just a fleck of tomato or a splash of wine can bring a missing dimension to a dish. Usually, when I taste something for salt, I consider acidity, too. The miracle a simple squeeze of lemon can create is not to be underestimated.

You do not always have to check acidity balance in an individual dish. Sometimes it is better to think of the whole plate. A tart relish or a little sparkling salad can lift a dish that on its own is good, but perhaps too rich or sweet or just needing a contrast.

There are times when you need to take an even bigger view, by looking at the meal as a whole. People like a mixture of taste experiences, so throwing a couple of zingy dishes into the mix is an easy way to bring some equilibrium to a menu. It is also possible simply to balance a meal with a glass of the right wine. It's something to bear in mind.

GARDEN PLOT BOUNTY

A T this time of year, soft fruit really comes into its own. Although we don't have a fig tree on our plot, the bicycle route home takes me past one that is heavily laden and spills its fruit onto the road. In the season I can't help but stop, no matter how heavily laden I already am. I also often make this recipe with blackberries only.

BURNISHED AUTUMN FRUIT

SERVES 6
vanilla bean, *1*
mascarpone, *1 cup*
egg yolks, *2*
sugar, *½ cup*
lemon juice, *a squeeze*
ripe figs, *6 or more*
raspberries, *2 cups*
blackberries, *2 cups*
slivered almonds, *2 tablespoons*

Preheat the oven to 350°F. Split the vanilla bean and scrape out the seeds. Mix the mascarpone with the vanilla seeds, egg yolks, sugar, and lemon juice.

Tear the figs in half and combine them with the raspberries and blackberries in a large, wide baking dish, arranging them in one layer. Spoon the mascarpone in a few blobs on top of the fruit. Sprinkle with the almonds.

Bake until the mascarpone has melted and turned a little brown, which only takes a few minutes. Now turn on the broiler and quickly broil, close to the heat source, until the top is just golden.

SHOOTS AND LEAVES SOUP

MAKE THIS WHEN YOU HAVE TOO MANY HOME-GROWN ZUCCHINI.
*It uses up the shoots and leaves, too. The recipe was mentioned to me in passing
by a friend with Sicilian roots. I'm not sure this is how his nonna made it,
but it tastes great. Feel free to use the recipe as a blueprint: you can use lots of
leaves with a few zucchini, or lots of zucchini with a few leaves. And add more
or less pasta. Just be sure that the garlic and chile are in sufficient quantity to
give the rest a bit of a punch.*

SERVES 4
tender zucchini shoots and smaller leaves, *about 1 pound*
zucchini, *4 (more or less)*
potato, *1*
good olive oil
garlic cloves, green shoot removed, minced, *2*
dried hot chile, crushed, *1*
tomato, quartered, *1 or 2*
pasta, broken into small pieces, *⅔ cup (more or less)*
zucchini blossoms, stamens removed, *a few*
oregano, *a few sprigs*

Wash the zucchini shoots and leaves well, then chop them up. Dice the
zucchini and potato pretty small. Heat up a good amount of olive oil in
a pan that will accommodate all your ingredients comfortably.

Fry the garlic until it is just turning brown. Add the dried chile
followed by the leaves, shoots, zucchini, tomato, and potato, and season.
Fry everything together briefly, then add water to just cover. Add the
pasta. Boil everything together rapidly until the pasta is cooked.

Add the zucchini blossoms and oregano, and check the seasoning.

Eat with a piece of toast that has been rubbed with a clove of garlic
and doused in good olive oil.

TOO MANY TOMATOES

This year I have managed to grow **loads of tomatoes**. Both the floating garden pontoon and the garden plot are laden with heavy fruits of all varieties. I love the smell of tomato plants and the sticky resin they leave on your hands.

Tomatoes are from the nightshade *(solanaceae)* family, an incredible group of plants that includes some of my favorite things—potatoes, tobacco, chiles, and eggplant—as well as wild nightshades both deadly and beautiful.

All tomatoes have different tastes and uses. Some, such as San Marzano, are better for sauces; others, like Amish Paste, are at their best roasted slowly. Some should be just sliced and eaten with salt and oil, such as green Costoluto Fiorentino, from Italy, and Tiger. I love to rub a piece of crunchy toast with cut garlic and then a soft ripe Datterini tomato, drizzle it with oil, and sprinkle with salt and dried wild oregano.

In general, I am not a preserver or pickler. Tomatoes, however, are a different matter. **I really love to use them all year round** and often spend a fortune on posh large jars of whole southern Italian preserved tomatoes. The really great thing about these is that they are kept in water instead of that horrible thick, sweet tomatoey stuff you get in a can. This year I am going to turn all my excess tomatoes into delicious sauce and put them in jars for the year.

*Having tomato sauce around
makes me very happy.*

AMISH PASTE

COSTOLUTO FIORENTINO

DATTERINI

COSTOLUTO FIORENTINO,
SLICED

TEARDROP

TIGER

GARDENER'S DELIGHT

SAN MARZANO

HOW TO MAKE REALLY GOOD TOMATO SAUCE

ALWAYS MAKE TOMATO SAUCE THIS WAY; IT IS THE BEST I'VE FOUND. *I use ratios rather than quantities, as it is intended to be adapted to however many tomatoes you have, and makes a sauce that can be put by in jars or eaten for dinner. It is a very useful recipe to have. And very nice indeed with pasta.*

ripe plum tomatoes (ideally San Marzano, or see recipe method)
garlic, *a big juicy clove for every 6 tomatoes*
olive oil
dried hot, red chile, *a tiny bit*
basil leaves, *handfuls*

Peel the tomatoes (see page 131). If you haven't grown any delicious San Marzano tomatoes, then you can use good canned—or even better, from jars—whole Italian plum tomatoes; rinse them to remove the horrible thick stuff they are usually covered in.

Cut the garlic in half lengthwise, and remove and discard the green sprouty bit. Slice the garlic thinly and evenly. Place a small, thick-bottomed pan over gentle heat. Pour in the oil, add the garlic, and fry until it starts to stick together. This sticky stage happens just before it starts to brown.

Add your tomatoes, a pinch each of salt and pepper, and the chile. Turn the heat right down, cover, and let cook for a long time, occasionally stirring and squashing any stubborn bits of tomato to break them up. After at least 1 hour, maybe 2, your sauce will be thickened, sweet, and delicious. Add a slug of good olive oil and a handful of basil if he's around; if not, marjoram or oregano will do. Make sure the sauce is well seasoned with salt.

Pour the boiling sauce into hot sterilized canning jars (a funnel will help). Tap the jars on your work surface to release any pockets of trapped air, then screw the lids on tightly. Process the sealed jars in a boiling-water bath for 30 minutes.

FATOUSH

THIS UBIQUITOUS LEBANESE SALAD IS TRULY AN AMAZING DISH.
It's even better if you use tomatoes and cucumbers you have grown yourself. Vary the ingredients with the season, but use only what is tasting good. You can buy sumac—a wonderful lemony spice—in Middle-Eastern markets. Choose your ingredients to represent a variety of textures and flavors. Lay them out and check the balance, then start chopping.

SERVES 2
pita bread, *1*
olive oil, *for drizzling*
small hothouse cucumber, chopped, *1*
ripe tomatoes, deseeded and chopped, *2*
radishes, chopped, *4*
celery heart, chopped, *1*
soft sweet herbs (such as dill, parsley, mint, fennel, cilantro), minced, *about ¼ cup*
soft, salty, white Arab cheese, which is a bit like feta, or feta itself, crumbled, *3 ounces*
lemon, *1*
sumac, *½ teaspoon*

Preheat the oven to 350°F. Tear the pita into pieces. Drizzle with oil and bake until hard and crunchy, about 5 minutes.

Mix all the vegetables, herbs, cheese, and bread together. Check the balance of ingredients: the salad should look pretty and be green from herbs. Douse in oil, squeeze the lemon juice over, and sprinkle with salt and sumac. Taste: the salad should be zingy and vibrant. If it isn't add more salt and lemon juice.

RASAM

A WONDERFUL THIN, SOUR, AND HOT SOUP FROM SOUTH INDIA. *Often served on the side of a lunch of rice and curry, it relies on sweet, ripe tomatoes to balance the sour tamarind.*

SERVES 6

tamarind pulp, *a golfball-sized piece*
cumin seeds, *¾ teaspoon*
garlic cloves, green sprout removed, *2*
fresh ginger, chopped, *1-inch piece*
black peppercorns, *1 heaping teaspoon*
ground turmeric, *¼ teaspoon*
hot chile powder, *½ teaspoon*
fresh curry leaves, *12*
coriander seeds, *1 heaping teaspoon*
asafetida (optional), *a small pinch*
vegetable oil, *a little*
mustard seeds, *1 heaping teaspoon*
large, ripe tomatoes, roughly chopped, *4*
sugar, *to taste*
lime juice, *to taste*
cilantro leaves, *a few*

Soak the tamarind pulp in 1 cup hot water for 10 minutes, then push the thick paste through a strainer, leaving behind the pits and stringy bits. Toast the cumin seeds in a dry frying pan for a few minutes until they smell aromatic.

In a large mortar and pestle, crush together the garlic, ginger, cumin seeds, peppercorns, turmeric, chile powder, curry leaves, coriander seeds, and asafetida (if using) with some salt until quite smooth.

Heat a deep, medium-sized saucepan and add a generous amount of oil to cover the bottom. Throw in the mustard seeds. As soon as they start to crackle, add the garlic and spice paste. Reduce the heat and fry a little until the garlic smells cooked. Don't let anything burn. Tip in the tomatoes and continue to cook on medium heat, adding the strained tamarind paste. Taste and adjust the seasoning, adding a little sugar or a squeeze of lime if needed. Scatter cilantro leaves on top and serve in little cups or glasses.

FRIED GREEN TOMATOES

IF YOUR TOMATOES REFUSE TO RIPEN, YOU CAN EAT THEM GREEN.
*Dip them in batter and deep-fry, along with squash blossoms—or marigold
flowers, which are just as delicious as squash blossoms.*

SERVES 4
for the tomatoes
large, green tomatoes, *3*
squash blossoms or marigold flowers, *8*
oil, *for deep-frying*

for the batter
all-purpose flour, *1½ cups*
beer, *1¼ cups*

for the mayonnaise
basil, *a handful*
salt, *a pinch*
lemon juice, *to taste*
egg yolk, *1*
extra-virgin olive oil, *⅔ cup*

Slice the green tomatoes about ½-inch thick. Remove the stamens from
the squash blossoms, or cut any hard parts from the marigolds, leaving
only tender shoots.

Sift the flour into a mixing bowl. Slowly pour in the beer, whisking, to
make a batter with the thickness of heavy cream. Put your finger in to
check the consistency; the batter should form a thin layer.

In a mortar and pestle, crush the basil with the salt until it is pretty
much a paste. Squeeze in a little lemon juice and add the egg yolk.
Continue to pound quickly while you slowly add the extra-virgin olive
oil. If you end up with a separated oil mixture, remove it from the
mortar, wipe that out, and start again with another egg yolk, adding the
split mixture slowly as if it were olive oil.

Heat about 1 inch of oil in a deep pan. Dip the tomatoes and
blossoms into the batter and tap against the bowl to remove excess, then
deep-fry until light brown and crunchy. Don't fry too many at a time.
Drain on paper towels and serve with the mayonnaise.

A WONDERFUL DINNER AFTER A HARD DAY'S WORK

I N the absence of an Indian tandoor oven, I cook my chicken on the barbecue. It's best to spatchcock the bird (this only takes a few minutes if you know how): split it open by cutting down either side of the backbone, using a sharp, heavy knife or poultry shears to cut through the bones. Press on the breastbone to flatten the bird and use a couple of metal skewers to keep it in shape.

TANDOOR CHICKEN

SERVES 2 VERY HUNGRY PEOPLE
cumin seeds, *2 heaping teaspoons*
coriander seeds, *2 heaping teaspoons*
cinnamon stick, *¾-inch piece*
black peppercorns, *1 teaspoon*
ground turmeric, *½ teaspoon*
Kashmiri (mild) chile powder, *2 heaping teaspoons*
small red onion, *1 slim wedge*
garlic cloves, green sprout removed, *4*
fresh, large, mild red chiles, deseeded and minced, *2*
plain yogurt, *1 cup*
smallish chicken, spatchcocked, *1*

Toast the cumin seeds in a dry pan over low heat until they smell slightly smoky and start to crackle. Tip into a large mortar (you could use a blender, but it's not as good). Add the coriander seeds, cinnamon, and peppercorns and grind to a fine powder. Add the turmeric, chile powder, onion, garlic and a generous amount of salt. Pound and grind to a fine paste. Mix in the chiles and yogurt. Rub the paste all over the chicken and let marinate at room temperature for a few hours.

Get the charcoal fire ready, spreading out the coals so it is not too hot. Lay the chicken as flat as you can and grill on both sides until cooked through. Pay particular attention to the legs.

Eat with Naan (see right), lime pickle, and cold beer.

NAAN

THESE BREADS ARE TRADITIONALLY COOKED IN A TANDOOR OVEN. *They are slapped onto the hot sides where they stick and bake. I think they are just as good grilled over hot coals.*

MAKES 6
active dry yeast, *1½ teaspoons*
all-purpose flour, *5 cups*
fine salt, *about 1 teaspoon*
plain yogurt, *3 tablespoons*
oil or ghee, *about 6 tablespoons*

Put the yeast in a small bowl with ½ cup warm water and set aside for 10 minutes.

Put the flour in a big bowl and add the salt, yogurt, and oil or ghee. Pour in the yeasty water and mix, then add another ½ cup warm water—a little more or a little less—to make a soft, elastic dough. Knead it very well, then cover the bowl tightly with plastic wrap and let rise for an hour.

Punch down, then shape the dough into six balls. Let rise again on a tray, covered with a damp dish towel.

When the time comes for cooking the bread, push each ball into a round about ½-inch thick. Grill on a coolish part of the barbecue for a couple of minutes on each side.

In October, as the air cools and becomes just a little more damp, you can almost feel the mushrooms growing. It is at this time of year that I take every opportunity to head for the woods in search of them. I am often disappointed, but I persevere in my chase for the elusive fungi, which are such an excellent prize on the rare occasions when I do find them (see page 152).

Many books contain instructions for making stock. It often seems that to be taken seriously as a cook, you have to have an enormous pot of bones forever bubbling on your stove. But I have never found this to be the case. For me, stock is excellent in itself—less a commodity and more a luxury. It's interesting to see how universal it is to make stock, and how different cultures have their own ways both of making it and of using their broths (see page 146).

MAKING STOCK...

... is easy, but takes a while. The technique may change a little from country to country, but most agree that the best way to extract flavor and goodness is by simmering flavorful things for a long time. Mostly bones.

Like most people, I don't make stock at home that often. I rarely use it casually—if I am going to make some, it tends to feature in what I'm cooking. Otherwise I use water and get flavor from a well-cooked base such as browned meat or dried mushrooms, or by adding a splash of wine. Only restaurants have huge pots of stock available. To be honest, I like using water; it tastes of nothing, which is often just what you want.

I certainly don't regard the stockpot as the garbage can of the kitchen. I can't imagine why anyone would want to put every bit of onion peel and carrot scraping, plus bones from people's plates, into a pot and boil it. And then, even worse, to make that thing called "jus." Chefs love jus and always put it on meat. Jus is really reduced stock, often veal, and tastes—at least to me—like Marmite water. It is the main reason why I avoid fancy French restaurants.

Stock is often made by accident. If you boil a chicken or some beef with carrots, celery, bay, fennel seeds, and peppercorns, you'll have the most delicious broth that you can practically drink on its own. This broth can then be flavored in different ways. For example, adding rice, star anise, dried scallops, bean sprouts, and cilantro makes it a delicious Chinese soup. Reducing it a little with a few more aromatic herbs makes it a lovely *brodo* for risotto.

If I am making stock on purpose I buy ingredients specifically for it: good free-range chicken carcasses, bits of beef bone with a little meat, and a pig's foot or two are always welcome in my pot. I rarely use much onion, but always add celery, black peppercorns, fennel seeds, chile, and bay. I never make stock with roasted bones; I find the "brown" flavor unwelcome.

Asian stocks are delicious. The master stocks of China are fantastic; they keep them on the go for a while, adding duck or pork, noodles, and vegetables as need dictates. Japanese stock—dashi—takes only minutes to make, but is a pure refinement of the complex qualities of tuna and seaweed.

Making fish stock is different from chicken and meat stocks. For example, it musn't be cooked for a long time (the only exception is the delicious stock you get when you boil an octopus for hours until tender). Also, you must choose your bones carefully. Bones and heads from flat, white fish are best—stock made from turbot or halibut is really fabulous and that from sole is very good. Bones from oily fish will not make an acceptable stock, but crab and lobster shells will add wonderful flavor. Be sure the bones are fresh and well washed (fish blood has a bitter, unpleasant taste).

I start by making a *soffritto* of sweet vegetables (see page 182), such as fennel, celery, and carrot, plus a little onion and garlic, then add the fish bones and half a bottle of wine. I cook off the alcohol, then cover with water and add the aromatic herbs I have to hand, a couple of tomatoes, and a piece of dried porcini. Cover and simmer for 20 minutes, then strain.

BONES AND BROTHS

THERE *are great restorative breakfasts all over the world, and this salty broth will cure most problems in life. When visiting Bangkok, I found an open-fronted restaurant near our guest house that housed big silver pots full of delicious and nutritious beef bone broth. The place had serried tiers of busy tables and at the front was a tea-making man, well established, in a special tea-making shack. His staple was pots of Chinese tea that were sometimes hot but often cool for drinking with ice. We always had our breakfast there. Once the beef bone broth is ready, this soup doesn't take long to make.*

PHO (BEEF BROTH NOODLE SOUP)

SERVES 4

beef shank or knuckle bones, *4*
pig's foot, *1*
black peppercorns, *a few*
Szechuan peppercorns, *a few*
celery ribs, *4*
star anise flowers, *2*
cinnamon stick, *¾-inch piece*
onion, halved, *1*
fresh ginger, *a thumb-sized piece*
fresh, large chiles, *2*
beef shank meat or brisket, *5 ounces*
fish sauce, *to taste*
garlic cloves, green sprout removed, evenly sliced, *4*
flavorless oil, *a splash*
cellophane noodles, *1 bunch for each bowl*
lovage (optional), *a few leaves for each bowl*
celery leaves, *a handful*
Swiss chard or spinach, shredded, *7 ounces*
cilantro leaves, *from 1 small bunch*

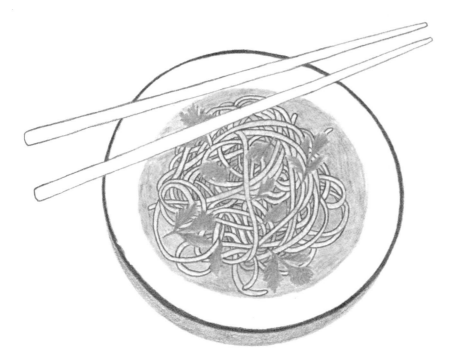

Cover the bones and pig's foot with water in a stockpot and add the peppercorns, Szechuan peppercorns, celery, star anise, cinnamon, onion, ginger, and chiles. Put on the lid and simmer gently for a day or so (about 8 hours), skimming regularly at first so the broth turns out clear. Put in the beef shank meat or brisket about 3 hours before you want to eat. Season the broth either with fish sauce alone or with fish sauce and salt.

Fry the garlic in the oil until deep golden brown, then spread on paper towels to cool. Boil the noodles briefly in the broth with the lovage, celery leaves, and chard or spinach, then remove with a slotted spoon and put into four bowls. Ladle some broth into each bowl and add pieces of meat. Sprinkle the crisp garlic and cilantro leaves on top. Eat with chopsticks and a big, flat metal spoon.

In Bangkok, they served wide bowls of this soup that were nicely small so the noodles never became soggy. People would often have two bowlsful. Offer dried chile flakes and fish sauce on the table.

BIRRIA

I ATE THIS DELICIOUS BROTH IN TLACOLULA, NEAR OAXACA, MEXICO. *There is an incredibly vibrant market there that is the size of a town. It is a busy area where people sit on benches at long tables and you buy this dish from whichever stall looks best, or whichever has the meat you prefer (Birria can be made with pork, goat, or lamb). Enjoy with a glass of mezcal añejo tequila, or a nice Mexican beer.*

SERVES 6

dried, smoked Mexican chiles, a mixture if possible, *5 ounces*
head of garlic, *1*
whole tomatoes, drained and rinsed, *14-ounce can*
pork shank on the bone, ideally with the foot, well cleaned, *1*
cider vinegar, *1 cup*
black peppercorns, *1 teaspoon*
wild oregano, *a pinch*
allspice berries, *1 teaspoon*
bay leaves, *6*
corn tortillas, *12*
cilantro leaves, *½ bunch*
scallions, thinly sliced, *2*
lime wedges, *for serving*

Cut the stalks from the smoked chiles and shake out the seeds. Soak them in 1½ cups boiling water for about 10 minutes. Meanwhile, peel all the garlic cloves and remove the green sprout from their centers. Put the chiles, tomatoes, and garlic in a food processor and blend to form a smoothish paste.

  Put the pork in a big pan and pour in the vinegar and the chile mixture. Add the peppercorns, oregano, allspice, and bay. Season well with salt. Pour in enough water to cover the pork and set over low heat. Cover and cook until the pork is completely tender, about 2 hours.

  When ready to eat, steam the tortillas wrapped in a dish towel, or according to the package directions.

  Serve with the tortillas, cilantro leaves, scallions, and lime wedges.

CAMBODIAN CHICKEN SOUP

I FOUND THIS AFTER GETTING LOST FOR HOURS ON A MOTORBIKE.
We were in the south of Cambodia, looking for a hidden beach while avoiding bandits and sunburn and attempting to survive the incredibly bumpy roads. This was offered somewhere along the way. Very pleased we were. You might think this sounds like gruel. But trust me—it is a real find.

SERVES 6
whole chicken (just some legs would be nice, too), *1*
scallions, *1 bunch*
star anise, *4*
cloves, *4*
fresh, hot chile, *1*
garlic, *1 head*
black pepper (preferably Kampot)
short-grain rice, such as jasmine, *1 cup*
flavorless oil, *a splash*
bean sprouts, *4 handfuls*
cilantro, *1 bunch*

Submerge the chicken in a pot of cold water and add the scallions, spices, some of the garlic cloves, salt, and lots of pepper. Simmer gently for about 1 hour, when the chicken will have flavored the broth nicely. Add the rice and keep cooking until the rice is really soft.

Meanwhile, slice the rest of the garlic very fine and fry it in the oil until deep golden brown, but not burned. Spread it out immediately on paper towels to cool.

When the rice is done, serve your soup by spooning some rice and plenty of the broth into each bowl. Shred a little pile of chicken into the bowl, set a handful of bean sprouts on top with some cilantro leaves, and scatter the fried garlic over.

I FOUND SOME PORCINI!

It is an amazing feeling to find a little family of porcini mushrooms (which are also called cèpes), although I am never one to complain about any edible wild mushroom I come upon. Do remember that you must take great care to ensure that any mushrooms you gather from the wild are edible.

There are many ways to enjoy your prized porcini:

– *They will make the best risotto, or the nicest topping for toast you may ever eat (see page 154).*
– *Put them on wet polenta, or eat them with a steak.*
– *Slice them and bake with potatoes or a piece of fish.*
– *If the mushrooms are small, firm, and round, they don't need to be cooked at all (see page 154). Squeeze the stem to check that it is resilient, and examine the cap to be sure it is not slimy.*
– *When you slice the mushrooms, you may find there are little maggots. This is a hazard you have to accept, and apparently not bad for you even if eaten raw.*
– *Larger, more developed mushrooms are better suited to cooking. When they are still firm I love to roast them whole (see page 155).*

Porcini have an amazing flavor that in some dishes can be incredibly delicate and in others very strong. Being rich in umami (see page 30), porcini are often used—particularly when dried—as a seasoning in many Italian dishes, to further intensify the flavor (see page 155).

RAW PORCINI SALAD

IT'S WORTH INVESTING IN REALLY GOOD, AGED PARMESAN FOR THIS. *Although it makes the dish expensive, the salad is only worth eating if all the items on the plate are as rare and delicious as the porcini. You will need extremely fresh mushrooms, so this is ideal as an early lunch to follow a morning spent foraging.*

SERVES 4
small porcini, *4*
good Parmesan, *4 ounces*
thyme leaves, minced, *½ teaspoon*
lemon juice, *to taste*
good olive oil, *to taste*

Wipe the caps of the mushrooms with a damp cloth and brush the stems clean. (Never wash or, worse, soak any kind of fresh mushroom in water; they will drink it up and become flabby in texture and diluted in taste.) Slice the mushrooms very thinly and lay them flat on a plate, as you would slices of beef in a carpaccio. Shave the Parmesan into thin but uneven shavings all over the mushrooms. Sprinkle with the thyme. Squeeze lemon juice over and pour on some good olive oil. Season with a little salt and pepper.

PORCINI ON TOAST
This is less of a recipe and more of a recommendation as to the best way to eat your first delicious porcini. Slice them thickly and frazzle them in butter until soft and brown, adding some minced garlic and parsley toward the end. Thick slices of very buttery toast are the best vehicle for this treat.

ROASTED PORCINI

THIS IS PERHAPS ONE OF THE BEST RECIPES FOR PORCINI THERE IS. *Just scale it up or down, depending on how many guests you have, or how many porcini you found.*

> **porcini,** *1 per person, or more if you have gathered a lot of mushrooms*
> **bacon or pancetta,** *1 or 2 slices per mushroom*
> **garlic cloves, green sprout removed, thinly sliced,** *a couple per mushroom*
> **thyme,** *a few sprigs*

Clean the mushrooms by wiping the caps with a damp cloth and peeling the stems with a vegetable peeler. Preheat the oven as hot as it will go.

Wrap each mushroom in a slice of bacon or pancetta; if the mushroom is particularly big, use a slice on the cap and another on the stem. Tuck a couple of slices of garlic and a few leaves of thyme into each piece of bacon as you wrap it around.

When you have wrapped all the mushrooms, put them in a baking pan where they will fit snugly. Sprinkle pepper over them, then roast until the bacon is crisp and the mushrooms soft and lightly browned, 6–15 minutes, depending on size.

Drink a glass of good Chianti with these.

HOW TO DRY FRESH PORCINI

If you have found more porcini than you can eat, you are very lucky indeed. To dry them, slice them ¼-inch thick and put them on a wire rack above a radiator or other warm place. When they are dry, keep them in a jar or a plastic bag.

A MALAYSIAN BREAKFAST FOR FRIENDS FROM PARIS. IT TOOK SO LONG TO MAKE, IT WAS MORE LIKE LUNCH. WAS WORTH IT, THOUGH ...

I LIKE to imagine that I am disorganized because I am creative—I am sure that you cannot be both creative and organized. So, when making this fabulous breakfast, I started it late and then didn't have enough time to get everything together. We had some toast with butter and eventually ate the "breakfast" for lunch. It was delicious all the same.

NASI LEMAK

THIS IS THE CLASSIC BREAKFAST EVERYWHERE IN SOUTHEAST ASIA. It is usually wrapped in banana leaf to make individual triangular packages. I was always pleased to see them on tables outside a cafe. You can use whatever mixture of hot and mild chiles suits you, but don't be too timid with them. Dried anchovies can be found in Indian and Thai markets.

FOR THE SAMBAL IKAN BILIS (DRIED ANCHOVY-CHILE SAUCE)

HERE'S THE UBIQUITOUS, WONDERFUL CHILE SAUCE OF MALAYSIA. *You can eat it with lots of different Malaysian things.*

SERVES 4
fresh red chiles, *5 ounces*
garlic cloves, green sprout removed, *4*
very tiny shallots, *6*
dried shrimp paste, *1 teaspoon*
palm sugar or brown sugar, *2 teaspoons*
dried anchovies, *2 ounces*
vegetable oil, *7 tablespoons*
red onion, thinly sliced, *1*
tamarind pulp, mixed with water to make a paste, *1 tablespoon*

In a mortar and pestle, grind together the chiles, garlic, shallots, shrimp paste, and sugar until pastelike.

In a small wok or pan, fry the anchovies in the oil until dark and crisp. Remove them to some paper towels. Discard most of the oil from the pan, leaving about 2 tablespoons. Fry the ground chile paste quickly in the oil, stirring, for 2 minutes. Add the onion and cook for 2 minutes longer. Next, add the tamarind water and some salt. Taste and adjust the sugar and salt: the sauce should be clearly salty, sweet, hot, and sour, as well as spicy. Return the anchovies and cook until the sambal is thick and dark brown.

FOR THE OTHER PARTS

EAT SOME OR ALL OF THESE WITH PLAIN RICE AND SPICY SAMBAL.

cold roast fish, *a small piece*
small hothouse cucumber, peeled and sliced, *1*
eggs, hard-cooked and halved, *4*
peanuts roasted in their skins, *a large handful*
banana, sliced and deep-fried until crisp, *a small pile*

Serve all of these extraordinary things around a mound of warm rice. With the sambal, it makes a surprising and delicious breakfast.

11

With the first frosts of the year, game birds put on a little fat and
start to taste better. This is the best time to eat them, before the
celebrations of December interrupt matters in the kitchen.
Apples, pears, and quinces are going strong now. At this time of
year I can eat a few apples a day but rarely cook them, preferring
instead the beautiful deep red of a roasted quince (see page 160).
Vietnamese sandwiches (see page 172)—traditional baguettes filled
with slow-cooked pork, pickles, and chile—are both unusual and
delicious. At first a seemingly strange concept, the baguette was in
fact institutionalized by French colonialists. In Vietnam, you often
buy them through the window of a rickety bus as you travel down
a dusty, uneven road.

BEAUTIFUL DOWNY QUINCES

Quince is an ancient fruit, and tastes like it. You can imagine the Romans eating quince; in fact, there are records of them stewing quinces with honey, which must have been quite lovely. The fruit probably comes from the Middle East and there you will find a few savory recipes using quince (these really don't appeal to me, because slow-cooked meat with fruit is not my favorite combination).

Quinces are beautiful, large, perfumed fruits that, when cooked for a long time, turn a deep, luxurious burnt red or orange color. The color becomes more intense—and increasingly stunning—the longer they cook.

The fruit is often made into jams, jellies, and preserves, such as quince paste, which the Spanish call membrillo. My family loves quince jelly with roast lamb—my mom makes it with fruit grown at my grandpa's house, adding twigs of rosemary.

When I worked at the restaurant Moro in London, we used to make a version of aioli with quince: crush some garlic, add some quince paste, then slowly pour in oil. It's wonderful with roast pork.

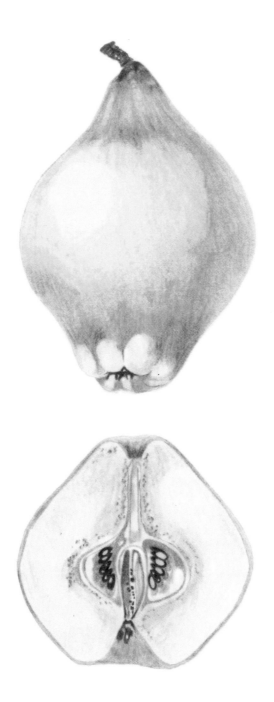

A KIND OF COARSE QUINCE PASTE

THIS IS QUINCE PASTE IN THE STYLE OF SPANISH MEMBRILLO.
It is great on buttered toast, as well as with a piece of Manchego cheese and a glass of fino sherry. Also try putting a bit inside a game bird when you roast it. The paste keeps well and makes a good gift.

    large quinces
    sugar

Preheat the oven to 350°F. Put the quinces in a roasting pan and add 1 inch of water, then completely seal the pan with foil. Bake for 2 hours. Remove from the oven and let cool.

Pull the quinces apart, removing the really tough bit in the middle of the fruit. Keep the skin and any other bits that aren't too hard. Measure the volume of quince flesh, along with any liquid from the pan, then put it in a heavy-based pan with the same (or a little less) volume of sugar. Set the pan over low heat and stir occasionally until the paste is a deep red color, about 1 hour. Be careful not to let the paste burn as it gets thicker. If it starts to stick, remove from the heat and cool a bit.

When the paste is ready, pour it into a tray lined with parchment paper and let cool and set. Cut into 6-inch slabs and wrap in parchment paper, tied with string. Keep in an airtight box.

BAKED QUINCE

    SERVES 2–4
    large quinces, *2*
    white wine, *½ bottle*
    sugar, *¾ cup*
    cinnamon stick, *1*
    bay leaves, *10*
    cloves, *4*
    fresh ginger, chopped, *a thumb-sized piece*

Preheat the oven to 300°F.

Peel and core the quinces, then cut into wedges. Put all the ingredients in a baking pan and completely seal with foil. Bake until tender, 1–2 hours. Eat with whipped cream or ice cream.

QUINCE CRISP

IF YOU HAVE A FAVORITE CRISP TOPPING RECIPE, USE IT INSTEAD. *I like mine, but am no granny-like authority on the matter.*

SERVES 4–6, DEPENDING ON APPETITE OR GREED

for the quinces
large quinces, *4*
sugar, *1 cup*
bay leaves, *a few*
ground ginger, *a sprinkle*

for the crisp topping
butter, *¾ cup + 2 tablespoons (1¾ sticks)*
self-rising flour, *2 cups*
rolled oats (if you have them), *a big handful*
light brown sugar, *¾ cup packed*

Preheat the oven to 325°F. Peel the quinces and cut each into six wedges. Remove and discard the core. Put the fruit in a baking dish that holds them comfortably. Add the sugar, bay leaves, and enough water just to cover. Bake until tender and red, 1–2 hours. (You can bake them for less time, but you'll won't get the beautiful color.) Remove from the oven and drain off a little of the liquid if there's a lot. Pick out the bay. Check the sweetness and add more sugar if you like. Mix in the ginger.

Increase the oven temperature to 375°F. To make the crisp topping, rub the butter and flour together until it resembles coarse crumbs. Work quickly and don't make it too fine. Toss in the oats and add the sugar, to taste, bearing in mind how sweet you have made your quince. Sprinkle the crisp on top of the fruit and bake until cooked through and the top is browned, about 40 minutes.

Eat with a big dollop of whipped cream.

A FISH FEAST: BOUILLABAISSE

THERE'S a lot of talk about what constitutes an authentic bouillabaisse. Some say that you can't cook it anywhere but in the south of France. Others say that if you don't have rascasse (scorpion fish) it is not a real bouillabaisse… that lobster is either a necessity or a sacrilege… that it must include wine or that it mustn't… In my opinion, what is really important when making bouillabaisse is to include a great variety of very fresh fish. It's an opportunity to use some of the cheaper, more plentiful types that are not endangered. Try to get a good balance between oilier fish and flaky white fish. Think of some of the smaller, bony fish as giving great flavor to the broth. In my restaurant I only use fish brought freshly caught to me each morning. This rules out fish from the Mediterranean, but I see no reason why I cannot call my saffron-laced, tomato fish stew flavored with wild herbs and served with rouille a bouillabaisse. I don't put wine or orange peel in my version, though they are common. This dish is a real event, and it is important to make it for a large number of people—at least 10—so you can use a good variety of fish.

SERVES AT LEAST 10

for the bouillabaisse
octopus, *1 weighing about 2¼ pounds*
garlic cloves, green sprout removed, *5*
fennel seeds (preferably wild),
  2 teaspoons
black peppercorns, *1 teaspoon*
a good balance of whole, fresh fish,
  cleaned, *9 pounds*
cayenne pepper, *a sprinkle*
olive oil
very small, live crabs (optional), *a few*
red onions, finely diced, *2*
fennel bulbs, finely diced, *2*
whole tomatoes, drained and rinsed,
  4 14-ounce cans
saffron threads, *a few pinches*

wild fennel herb (optional), *a little*
large waxy potatoes, *2¼ pounds*
fresh mussels, cleaned, *8 ounces*

for the rouille
saffron threads, *a pinch*
garlic cloves, green sprout removed, *2*
anchovy fillets, *4*
egg yolks, *2*
soft bread crumbs, *2½ cups*
good olive oil, *⅔ cup*

for the croutes
baguette, thinly sliced and dried out
  in the oven, *1*

Put your octopus in a big pot, cover with water, and add 2 garlic cloves, 1 teaspoon fennel seeds, and the peppercorns. Cover with a lid and set over medium-low heat.

Now, prepare your collection of fish. It's best to leave them whole, although sometimes I cut them into chunks straight through the bone. Grind the remaining garlic cloves and fennel seeds with the cayenne. Stir in a little olive oil. Rub this mixture all over the fish. Set aside.

After about an hour, check to see if the octopus is tender (cut it with a knife; it shouldn't be bouncy). If it is not, keep on cooking it gently. A fresh octopus often takes longer to cook than frozen, because the meat hasn't been tenderized by freezing. When the octopus is tender, remove it from the water and cut into small pieces, discarding any unsavory bits (I don't mind the suckers, but watch out for parts in the head).

Put the crabs into the octopus broth and boil gently for a few minutes, then remove them to a large mortar and pestle. Bash them up a bit to break the shells and release the flavor. Put them back in the pot and cook for 5 minutes longer. Strain the broth and discard the crabs.

Heat some olive oil in the pot and gently fry the onions and fennel until they are sweet and soft, about 15 minutes. Add the tomatoes and continue to cook gently for 30 minutes, stirring occasionally. Pour in the strained octopus–crab broth and simmer for 30 minutes longer. Strain the broth again, pushing as much of the vegetable mulch as you can through the strainer. Taste the broth: it should be rich and well-seasoned by the octopus and vegetables. You should have enough for a couple of bowls each. Sprinkle the saffron and wild fennel into the broth. Peel the potatoes and cut them into wedges. Boil them gently in the broth until tender.

Meanwhile, make the rouille. Soak the saffron in ½ cup of the hot fish broth. Crush the garlic with some salt in a mortar and pestle until smooth and white, then add the anchovy fillets and grind to a fine paste. Add the egg yolks and then the bread crumbs to the mortar, grinding to mix. Stir with the pestle while slowly adding the saffron liquid, then slowly pour in the olive oil, stirring all the time, to make a thick emulsion. Taste and adjust the balance of flavors: you may need more broth, oil, or salt, or a bit of cayenne, or vinegar or lemon. The rouille should be strong, because it will season the whole dish.

When the potatoes are done, remove them with a slotted spoon and put them in a warm dish. Cover with foil and leave in a warm place.

Add the fish to the broth in order of delicacy and expected cooking time. Start with the larger whole fish, then the smaller ones, then the mussels, cooking until they open. Add a good slug of olive oil.

Eat the broth first, with a croute or two spread with rouille. Then serve the fish with the potatoes and more broth on the side. With my bouillabaisse I like to drink a lightly chilled, young red wine from the south of France.

ALMOND AND JAM TART

THIS IS BASED ON THE RIVER CAFE'S ALMOND AND PEAR TART.
The pastry recipe here makes enough for two tarts, but it freezes well.

SERVES 6-8

for the pastry
all-purpose flour, *2⅓ cups*
unsalted butter, *1 cup (2 sticks)*
salt, *a pinch*
confectioners' sugar, *scant 1 cup*
egg yolks, *3*

for the almond paste
whole blanched almonds, *1⅔ cups*
all-purpose flour, *⅓ cup*
unsalted butter, softened, *1¼ cups (2½ sticks)*
sugar, *1¼ cups*
eggs, *3*

delicious jam (preferably homemade), *⅔ cup*

Start with the pastry. In a food processor, pulse the flour, butter, salt, and sugar together until the mixture forms fine crumbs. Add the egg yolks and pulse a bit more. Pour the crumbs onto a work surface and quickly bring together with your hands into a dough. Let rest in the refrigerator, wrapped in plastic wrap, for a couple of hours. Remove and freeze half the pastry for the next tart you make.

Preheat the oven to 300°F. Coarsely grate the chilled pastry into a 10-inch fluted tart pan. Quickly and firmly push the grated pastry against the sides and over the base to line. Keep it rough: don't work the pastry too much and don't worry about holes. Chill the tart shell in the freezer for 15 minutes until hard, then bake until firm and pale brown, about 15 minutes.

For the almond paste, roughly grind the almonds and flour in a food processor. Beat the butter and sugar together until smooth, then work in the almonds and, one by one, the eggs.

Spread the jam over the bottom of the tart shell, then smooth the almond paste on top. Bake until firm and golden, about 50 minutes.

THOUGHTS ON GAME

People often think that game birds are posh. I don't agree, unless of course it's a red grouse from Scotland, which is posh for good reason: it is very delicious. If you are ever lucky enough to try one, you'll discover that it has a delicate, subtle, and complex flavor, due to its diet of young heather in the wild.

Small game birds—partridges, grouse, quail, woodcock—should all be cooked in more or less the same way: roasted fast in a hot oven, with a few herbs inside, a nut of butter, and a glass of good wine sploshed in some time before the end of cooking. Most should be eaten a little rare. It is difficult to dictate cooking times for game birds. The best thing to do is squeeze their bottoms. First have a squeeze when they are raw; you'll find it's pretty squishy. As they cook, their bottoms firm up. Take them out when they're medium-firm, remembering that they will cook further while they rest.

Smaller game animals like hare are more suited to slow-cooking. When presented with a handsome hare to cook, I am most likely to tackle it by making a dish like Marcella Hazan's pappardelle alla lepre. This is a little less hard-core than the jugged hare that used to be a common dish in England, where the hare is cooked in its own blood. Generally I don't cook wild rabbits because they are often very lean and tough. Instead I opt for farm-raised rabbits with their delicate white meat that is happy in a biriani, or simply barbecued.

PHEASANTS ROSE GRAY

PHEASANTS CAN BE SLOW-COOKED OR ROASTED HOT AND FAST.
I often cook this dish, which I learned at the River Café from Rose Gray. It was one of the things she usually cooked herself—whether because she loved to make it or didn't trust anyone to make it like she did, I don't know. She certainly made it well. This is how I remember it—near the original, I hope. I often use a cheapish Chianti. Rose would probably have used something more elegant, such as Barolo.

SERVES 4
good pheasants, *2*
olive oil, *a generous splash*
small acorn squash, *1*
celery root, *1 small head*
celery heart, *1*
large waxy potatoes, *a few*
cinnamon sticks, *2*
sage, *1 bunch*
bay leaves, *2*
garlic cloves, green sprout removed, *6*
tomatoes, squeezed, *6*
fresh red chile, *1*
Italian red wine, *1 bottle*

Season the pheasants well inside and out. Brown them gently in oil in a pan that will hold them and the vegetables snugly. Peel the vegetables and cut into large wedges. Put them in the pan and add all the other ingredients, with some salt and a generous amount of black pepper.

Set the pan on a very gentle heat, cover, and cook for 1½ hours, or longer if the vegetables have not softened enough by then. A meal in itself, this needs nothing more, except perhaps a salad dressed with balsamic vinegar beforehand.

A PRETTY SERIOUS BREAKFAST

THE WOODCOCK IS A BEAUTIFUL BIRD, RARE AND HIGHLY ESTEEMED. *It is hunted but not sold, so you need to befriend a hunter to obtain one or two. You can eat the whole bird, including entrails (except the gizzard) and brains. This makes a hearty breakfast on a cold frosty morning—try it the Scottish way, with a little whisky in your cup of tea. If this is too much for you as a breakfast, it makes an amazing first course, perhaps with a glass of Barbera.*

SERVES 2
woodcocks, *2*
oil
butter or goose fat, *2 tablespoons*
large pieces of toast, *2*
sage, *a few leaves*

Preheat the oven to its highest setting. Prepare the birds by rubbing them with a little oil and seasoning well with salt and pepper. Make sure the feet are cut off and push the beak firmly through the tail. Put the birds in a small roasting pan with the butter or goose fat on top. Roast until starting to brown. Meanwhile, butter your toast.

Take the birds from the oven and slip the toast underneath, putting a few sage leaves in between.

Return to the oven and roast until the toast is crisp and the birds well browned. Take them from the oven, split the head in half with a sharp knife, and pull the entrails onto the toast. If everything looks a little undercooked, flash back into the oven for a little more roasting.

VIETNAMESE SANDWICHES (BANH MI)

I FIRST had Vietnamese sandwiches when I was traveling around Southeast Asia at age 16. I forgot about them until—when living in New York—we stayed in an apartment above Nicky's Vietnamese Sandwiches, a great shop in the Lower East Side. I loved them and would eat them often.

When making Vietnamese sandwiches, the most important thing—after buying good pork and a crunchy baguette—is the five-spice mix. Five-spice is found throughout Asia and its flavor depends on where it is made. You can also make these sandwiches with butterflied sardines, coated in flour and fried.

MAKES 10 SANDWICHES
(THE PORK KEEPS FOR A FEW
DAYS IN THE REFRIGERATOR)

for the five-spice
Szechuan peppercorns, *2 teaspoons*
star anise, *5*
cloves, *5*
cinnamon stick, *1-inch piece*
anise seeds, *1 tablespoon*
black peppercorns, *¼ teaspoon*
fennel seeds, *1 teaspoon*

for the meat
small, boned pork shoulder
 (Boston butt), *½*
cilantro, *1 bunch*
garlic cloves, minced, *3*
red onions, minced, *2*
fresh ginger, minced, *1-inch piece*
vegetable oil, *a splash*
fish sauce, *to taste*
rice wine vinegar, *a splash*

for the pickles
rice wine vinegar, *1 cup*
sugar, *to taste*
fresh ginger, *1 hand*
fish sauce, *to taste*
carrots, *2*
small daikon, *1*
red radishes, *1 bunch*
scallions, *1 bunch*
hothouse cucumbers, *1 large*
 or 2 smaller

for the sandwiches
butter
crunchy small baguettes, *as many*
 as you want sandwiches
fresh hot chiles, finely sliced,
 to taste

For the five-spice, toast the Szechuan pepper for a minute or so in a dry frying pan to freshen it up, then grind it vigorously with all the other ingredients in a mortar and pestle until very fine.

Coarsely grind the pork, or ask a friendly butcher to do this. Mince the stems of the cilantro; set the leaves aside. Brown the garlic, onions, ginger, and minced cilantro stems slowly in a little vegetable oil in a large, heavy pan. Add the meat and 2 teaspoons of the five-spice mix. Increase the heat and cook, stirring, until the pork is well browned. Splash in some fish sauce, then check the spice and salt. It should be very aromatic but not aggressively spiced. Add a little water and the rice wine vinegar, then cover with a circle of parchment paper and the lid. Cook, adding more water when necessary, until soft and sort of gloopy. This will take at least 1 hour.

To make the pickling liquid for the vegetables you need to get the right balance of vinegar, sugar, and salt. Start with two glasses of rice wine vinegar and one handful of sugar. Warm this with some of the same whole spices you put in your five-spice and a couple of small chunks of ginger. When the sugar has dissolved, taste the liquid. Generously add fish sauce for saltiness. Taste again and adjust the sweet and sour balance. The mixture should be salty enough to season the vegetables, and tart so the pickles will cut through the fattiness of the pork, but not mouth-scrunchingly so. Let cool a little.

Cut the carrots, daikon, red radishes, and scallions into long, thin strips, using a mandoline if you have one (watch your fingers). Cut the cucumbers into sixths lengthwise. Put the prepared vegetables into the just warm pickling liquid and leave for at least an hour, but no longer than overnight.

Now build your sandwich. Butter the baguette. Make a layer of the pork filling in it. Cover this with the drained, pickled vegetables, some fresh chile, and cilantro leaves.

December has always been the month for feasting. Whether we choose to celebrate a sacred tree, or the birth of the son of God, eating together is very important for both body (to keep warm) and soul (ditto) at this time of year. Though not a great fan of the traditional Christmas dinner, I love to share special meals with my family (see page 184), and we have come up with our own food traditions.

Giving people presents that you have both made yourself and that they can eat (see page 186) is particularly rewarding. Gifts like this are truly appreciated, and it gives you a cozy glow, too.

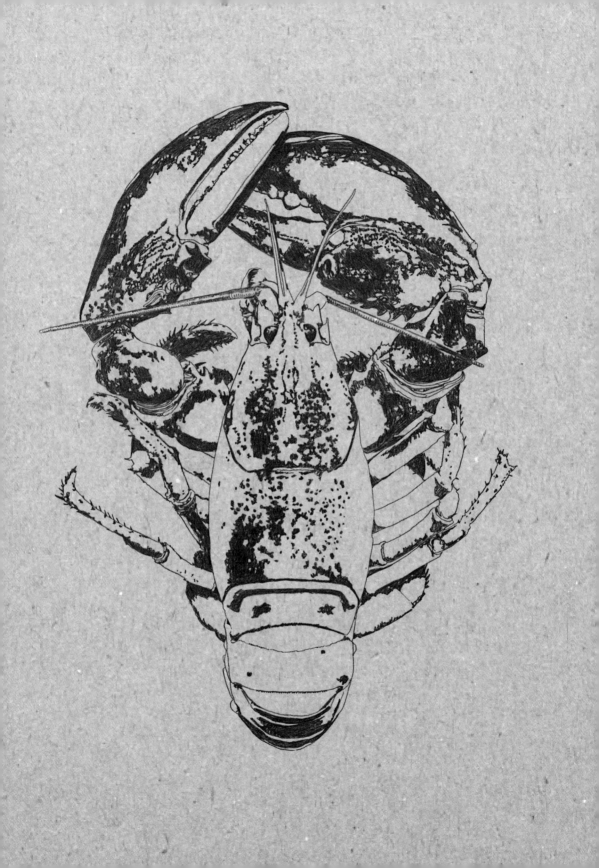

CLAMS IN WINTER

W HILE they are wonderful at other times of year, clams in winter seem to be particularly sweet. There are lots of different ways to cook them and none takes long. Basically, you throw them into a hot pan with all sorts of flavorings and some liquid, cover, and steam them open. It's good to experiment with the flavorings, because they always taste good. If you add clams to a fish stew or a piece of roasting fish, their umami-rich flavor lends great depth. Many clam recipes can also be used for mussels.

Make sure your clams are fresh and alive, with undamaged shells. Rinse them well in cold water. If you are worried about any of your hardshell clams, tap the shell; a strong, live clam will snap closed. Live softshell clams will move if touched.

CLAMS WITH ROMESCO SAUCE

SERVES 4
garlic cloves, green sprout removed, thinly sliced, 2
olive oil
fresh clams, 1 pound
white wine, a splash
Romesco Sauce (see page 36), a few spoons

Sauté the garlic in olive oil until soft but not colored, then throw in your clams and white wine. Cover the pan and steam until the clams open. Add the Romesco sauce and serve.

CLAMS WITH COCONUT AND CURRY LEAVES

SERVES 4

flavorless oil, *a few tablespoons*
mustard seeds, *1 teaspoon*
fresh curry leaves, *a few*
coconut, flesh coarsely grated (see page 73), *½*
fresh ginger, grated, *1-inch piece*
garlic cloves, green sprout removed, minced, *3*
dried hot chile, *2*
tomatoes, *4*
fresh littleneck clams, *1 pound*
lime, *1*

Heat a pan until hot. Add the oil, then throw in the mustard seeds, the
curry leaves, coconut, ginger, garlic, and chile. Tear in the tomatoes.
Add the clams along with a good squeeze of lime and a splash of water.
Put a lid on the pan and steam until the clams open.

CLAMS WITH TOMATO AND PORCINI

SERVES 4

dried porcini (see page 155), *¾ ounce*
garlic cloves, green sprout removed, thinly sliced, *2*
olive oil
whole plum tomatoes, drained and rinsed, *2 14-ounce cans*
fresh clams, *1 pound*
red wine, *a little splash*
toasted ciabatta, *4 pieces*

First soak the porcini in 1 cup boiling water for 30 minutes. Fry the
garlic in a little olive oil. When it starts to stick together—a moment
before it browns—add the drained porcini. Season with pepper and a
little salt and then, after a minute or so, add the tomatoes.

Cook over medium heat, breaking up the tomatoes, until the sauce
has thickened. Throw in the clams and red wine. Cover with a lid and
steam until the clams open.

Put the pieces of toasted ciabatta in four wide, flat soup bowls and
distribute the clams and sauce evenly among them.

CLAMS WITH CHICKPEAS AND DRIED OREGANO
Sauté a little garlic and dried hot chile in olive oil until soft
but not browned, then throw in your clams with a splash
of white wine. Cover and steam until open. Add cooked
chickpeas and a sprinkle of dried oregano.

CUTTING THE CAVOLO NERO

I love to go out on a frosty day to cut the cavolo nero. You can grow this cabbage all year, but—like most types—it makes the best eating after a good frost. The sharp cold seems to sweeten them up. Cavolo nero has an intriguing flavor that holds up well against lots of things, and is the traditional Tuscan accompaniment to fresh-pressed olive oil. This combination is really mind-blowingly good.

One of the best things to do with cavolo is to boil in well-salted water until soft, then chop and braise with fried garlic, fennel seeds, and chile. Liberally pour in more olive oil before eating.

BORTADELLO

SIMILAR TO RIBOLITTA, THIS IS TRADITIONALLY PREPARED ON SHIPS.

SERVES 6
red onion, *1*
celery heart, *1*
carrot, *1*
garlic cloves, green sprout removed, *3*
olive oil
tomatoes, *2*
cavolo nero, stripped from the stem, *1 pound*
borlotti (cranberry) beans, drained and rinsed, *14-ounce can*
polenta, *3 tablespoons*

Chop the onion, celery, and carrot coarsely and the garlic medium-fine.
Season well and cook gently in olive oil, stirring occasionally, in a heavy-
based saucepan until very soft, about 20 minutes. Add the tomatoes,
torn up a bit, and let cook a little more.

Coarsely chop the cavolo nero. Put it and the beans into the pot and
add 1 cup or so of water and the polenta. Cook until the cavolo is soft
and the polenta cooked, about 20 minutes. The soup should be thick.
Finish with a slug of good oil. Let the soup sit for a while before you eat
it—you want it nicely warm but not really hot.

CHRISTMAS EVE WITH IN-LAWS AND OUTLAWS

A N excellent dish for a celebration. I love to roast different meats together like this; they exchange flavors and help each other taste great. Most of the meats here are nice a little undercooked, but also delicious a little over. Just make sure they are flavored well and eaten as soon as they are ready.

It has become something of a tradition for my family and Nicky's family to have dinner together on Christmas Eve. There are often more distant relatives there as well, whether from Scotland or Zimbabwe. Whoever turns up, we always drink too much. We have had some fantastic meals, from Sri Lankan feasts to bouillabaisse, but this arrosto misto was especially successful.

I first tasted this dish on the excellent wine estate at Selvapiana in Chianti Rufina in Italy. They serve it on enormous silver platters with plain white beans soaked in their own delicious, bright green, just-pressed olive oil. That's how I serve it, too.

You can make the arrosto misto with a smaller variety of meats. It's great just with rabbit, sausage, and duck, for instance, though you should have a mixture of no less than three. In truth, you can use the meats you like, because, traditionally, it would have been made with whatever had been shot that day.

ARROSTO MISTO

YOU MIGHT WANT TO ASK THE BUTCHER TO PREPARE THE MEATS. *Or you can do it yourself. It's easy.*

SERVES 10
partridges, *3*
cured pork belly (pancetta or slab bacon), in one piece, *2¼ pounds*
fresh Italian sausages, *3*
hen pheasant, *1*
duck, *1*
farm-raised rabbit, *1*
garlic, *1 whole head*
sage, *a big bunch*
rosemary, *a big bunch*
tomatoes, *6*
fennel seeds, *a generous sprinkling*
olive oil
white wine, *2 glasses*

First prepare the meats (or ask the butcher to do it for you). With poultry shears, or a small, sharp knife, split the partridges in half by cutting through the backbone and breastbone; bisect each half just behind the thigh. Cut the pork and sausages into 1¼-inch cubes. Split the pheasant in half, then cut the drumstick from the thigh and cut each breast in two. Prepare the duck the same way, cutting the breast into three or four. Cut the front and hind legs from the rabbit; cut the hind legs in two, then divide the saddle into three or four pieces (discard the upper rib cage and back shins). Divide the garlic into cloves.

Preheat the oven to 400°F. Lay all the pieces of meat in one or two roasting pans that will hold everything snugly: the pieces should be in one layer and there should not be too much space between them. (This is important as it will really affect the cooking.) Tuck the garlic and the whole branches of herbs in around the pieces of meat. Tear up the tomatoes and tuck them in, too. Season well with salt, pepper, and fennel seeds. Moisten with some olive oil and the wine. Roast to the desired degree of doneness, 45 minutes to 1 hour. Check one of the larger pieces to see if it is cooked enough near to the bone.

This is good with white beans dressed with olive oil, potatoes roasted with garlic and rosemary, and greens such as cavolo nero (see page 179).

SOFFRITTO

Soffritto is one of the keys to really good cooking. This Italian base of mixed vegetables slow-fried in olive oil gives any dish depth and richness. Soffrito is not hard to prepare, but there are a few things you must do.

Firstly, choose your pan with care. You need one with a heavy base, which will distribute the heat evenly, meaning there aren't hot spots where the vegetables could burn. As well as being heavy, your pan must be the right size, because the ingredients need to steam a bit as well as fry.

Secondly, make sure the heat is really low, because the longer and slower you cook the base the better it will be.

Thirdly, to ensure the vegetables steam-fry properly, you need to season them, because salt will draw out a bit of moisture. And, of course, a well-seasoned base will flavor the dish really well. You shouldn't need to add water—if the temperature is low enough and the pan deep enough the soffrito will create its own steamy environment without any help.

The classic Italian soffritto consists of onion, carrot, and celery. Other cuisines have their own versions of soffrito, and include other vegetables and flavorings. For example, the Spanish sofrito, used as the base for paella, has all sorts of extras in it, including lots of bay, fresh and dried chiles, and garlic. It's cooked for ages and gives excellent flavor to the rice. In the Middle East, they add green herbs, such as parsley and celery leaves, to their bases. Many an Indian dhal or vegetable curry starts with onions slow-cooked with spices and herbs. Adding spices at the beginning of cooking toasts them slightly and begins to bring out their exotic flavors.

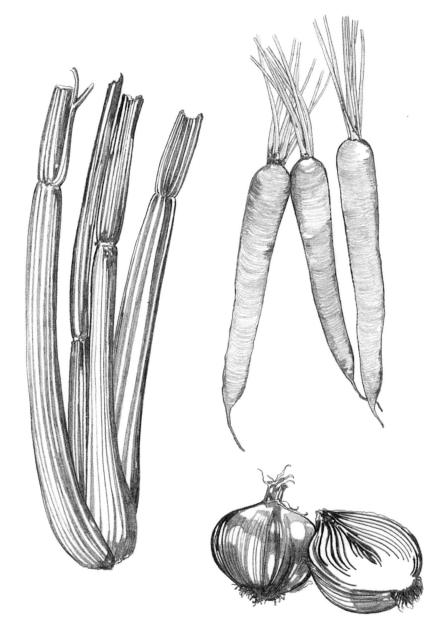

CHRISTMAS DAY FOR A FAMILY THAT DOESN'T REALLY LIKE CHRISTMAS DINNER

T O *say that my family doesn't really like Christmas dinner is not exactly true. In fact, it's me—I don't really like Christmas dinner, and I generally do the cooking.*

GRILLED LOBSTER

FIX YOURSELF A WARMING DRINK AND HEAD OUT INTO THE COLD. *It is great to light a barbecue in the winter. If the weather is just too bad, then you can cook the lobsters under the broiler.*

> large, live lobster, *1 each*
> dried hot chile, crumbled
> fennel seeds
> dried oregano
> coriander seeds, crushed
> lemon

Put the lobsters into the freezer for about 15 minutes so they become sleepy. Then, with a heavy, sharp knife, cut them down the middle from head to tail. Smash the claws up a bit.

Season the flesh well with all the dry flavorings listed (and salt and pepper, of course), then grill them, shell side down, for about 5 minutes. Turn them over and give them a bit of color on the flesh side. Remove and squeeze some lemon juice over.

THREE-TIMES-COOKED FRIES

IF YOU'RE GOING TO MAKE FRENCH FRIES AT HOME, DO IT LIKE THIS. *It's the best way. I use sunflower oil. You'll need a deep-fat thermometer.*

SERVES 6
potatoes, peeled and cut into thick fingers, *2 pounds*
oil of choice, *for deep-frying*

Put the potatoes in a pan of well-salted water and bring to a boil, then drain and dry well on paper towels. Heat the oil to 300°F. Fry the potatoes in the oil until completely soft. Remove from the pan.

Heat the oil to 375°F and fry the potatoes again until they are crisp and golden brown. Blot on paper towels and eat hot, with an interesting salad and some anchovy sauce (see page 28).

I LOVE TIRAMISU

YOU MUST HAVE GOOD ITALIAN COFFEE FOR THIS RICH DESSERT. *It makes all the difference.*

SERVES 4–6
freshly made espresso, *1 cup*
brandy, *1¼ cups*
savoiardi cookies or ladyfingers, *8 ounces*
eggs, separated, *2*
confectioners' sugar, *1 cup*
mascarpone, *2 cups*
hazelnuts, toasted and coarsely ground, *1½ cups*
unsweetened cocoa powder, *¼ cup*

Mix the coffee and brandy. Put the cookies in a dish (about 12 inches across). Pour the coffee mixture over them. Whisk the egg yolks and sugar with the mascarpone. In another bowl, beat the egg whites to soft peaks, then fold into the mascarpone. Spread evenly over the cookies. Sprinkle with the nuts and sift the cocoa powder over the top. Cover and refrigerate for 2 hours, then eat it.

PRESENTS YOU CAN EAT

I THINK *it is nice to give someone something you have made. Quince Paste (see page 162) and Preserved Lemons (see page 20) make nice presents, and here are a few more.*

CONSTANCE'S GINGER CAKE

THIS IS DELICIOUS AND LASTS A WEEK OR SO WRAPPED IN PAPER. *It's a 1950s British classic that fills the house with a delicious aroma as it bakes. Make it at least one day in advance of eating.*

SERVES 8-10
butter, plus more for the pan, ½ *cup (1 stick)*
light brown sugar, ½ *cup + 2 tablespoons packed*
golden raisins, *1 cup*
dark molasses, *1 cup*
ground ginger, *1½ tablespoons*
eggs, *2*
all-purpose flour, *1¼ cups*
baking soda, *½ teaspoon*
ground almonds, *⅔ cup*

Preheat the oven to 300°F. Put the butter, sugar, raisins, molasses, and 2 tablespoons water in a saucepan and bring to a boil. Boil for 5 minutes, then let cool.

Beat in the ginger and then the eggs, one at a time. Sift in the flour with the baking soda. Add the almonds and fold in well.

Turn the batter into a buttered and lined 8-inch square cake pan and bake for 1 hour. Cool on a wire rack.

NOUGAT

EACH TIME I MAKE THIS CONFECTION, THE RESULT IS DIFFERENT. *Sometimes it comes out hard, sometimes soft. But it is always good. To get a predictable result, you need to be little more scientific than I am, by using a candy thermometer. I prefer to let the nougat emerge the way it will. I use hazelnuts, but almonds or pistachios are fine, too. To finish, you can coat the nougat in chocolate, or put it between wafer cookies.*

> MAKES 24 SQUARES
> rice paper
> egg whites, *2*
> confectioners' sugar, *4 cups*
> liquid glucose or light corn syrup, *2 teaspoons*
> well-flavored honey, *¼ cup*
> hazelnuts, toasted and skinned, *1½ cups*

Line the bottom and sides of a 4 x 6-inch tray or pan with rice paper.

Beat the egg whites until they form soft peaks. Put the sugar, glucose, honey, and ¼ cup water into a small saucepan and stir over low heat until the mixture reaches 275°F on a candy thermometer, or until it turns crunchy when you drop a tiny bit into cold water.

Remove from the heat and slowly pour the hot sugar mixture onto the egg whites, beating all the time. Continue beating until the mixture is really glossy and pretty stiff.

Stir in the nuts. Spread the mixture over the rice paper in the tray. Cover with another piece of rice paper and press down with something flat to smooth out the nougat. Leave overnight until cold, then cut into 1-inch squares. Keep in an airtight box.

CANDIED FRUIT

IN GENOA, I VISITED ROMANENGO, AN ANCIENT CONFECTIONERS. *There they use huge copper cauldrons to make everything from crystallized cinnamon sticks to candied chestnuts and jellied rose-petal sweets. The heat under the vats of candied fruit is carefully regulated by passing hot water underneath. This process is quite easy to replicate at home over several days. You can candy almost any fruit, although harder fruit such as mandarins and other citrus, quinces, and pears are more successful than soft berries. I like to use a good tart fruit like lemon, plum, Seville orange, or loquat. The important thing when candying fruit is not to allow it to get too hot, because if it does the flavor changes significantly.*

     fruit
     sugar

Unless you are candying something big like a grapefruit, it is best to leave the fruit whole. Otherwise, cut it into big wedges.

Pierce the fruit all over with a toothpick, making deep holes about ½ inch apart. Mix equal volumes of sugar and water together, in sufficient quantity to cover the fruit. Warm to dissolve the sugar, then boil for a minute to stabilize the syrup. Pour the syrup into the top of a double boiler (or a bowl set over a pan of boiling water) and add the fruit. Heat over low heat for 4–5 hours, keeping the syrup at about 160°F. Let cool overnight.

The next day, heat in the same way for 4–5 hours.

On the following day, prepare a fresh syrup and transfer your fruit to it. Heat for another 4–5 hours. Repeat the day after that.

The fruit should now be ready, although check it by eating a bit: it should be chewy and as sweet as the syrup. If the fruit is done, remove it to a wire rack; if not, continue the candying process. At Romanengo, after candying they pass the fruit through a more crystallized syrup. You can make this by preparing another syrup and stirring it a lot as it cooks to make crystals form; these give the fruit a crunchy, glazed exterior. The process is a little tricky and I usually don't do it, but give it a try if you'd like. Depending on the fruit, the candying syrup can make a nice base for drinks.

KLAICHA

THESE DELICIOUS IRAQI PASTRIES MAKE A SUMPTUOUS PRESENT.
*Apparently, the prophet Mohammed said that black seeds will cure all ills
except death.*

MAKES ABOUT 20
all-purpose flour, *4⅓ cups*
salt, *a pinch*
confectioners' sugar, *½ cup*
butter, *1¼ cups (2½ sticks)*
rosewater, *1 tablespoon*
good-quality dates, pitted, *7 ounces*
blanched almonds, *½ cup*
egg yolk, *1*
milk, *a splash*
black seeds (nigella/kalonji), *2 tablespoons*

Sift the flour, salt, and sugar into a bowl. Rub in 1 cup of the butter,
then bring the dough together with the rosewater and a little water, if
necessary. Let the pastry rest in the refrigerator for a few hours.

Fry the dates in the remaining butter, adding a splash of water
and breaking them up with the back of a wooden spoon to make a
smoothish paste. Preheat the oven to 350°F.

Roll out the pastry until very thin (less than ¼-inch thickness) and cut
into rounds about 6 inches in diameter. Put a little date mixture in the
middle of each round and push an almond into it. Fold the pastry over
to make a little half-moon. Pinch the edges to seal them well. Repeat
with the pastry trimmings.

Mix the egg yolk with the milk, and paint this onto each pastry using
a brush. Sprinkle with a few black seeds. Bake until golden brown,
about 15 minutes.

INDEX

I WOULD LIKE TO THANK...

Rose, Ruthie, Sam and Sam, Skye, April, Darina, Jomundo, Sian, and all the other people who have, and still do, teach and inspire me to cook better.

Anne Furniss for believing in me and Lucy Bannell for her support and patience. Elly and Heather for making me presentable. Ros Shiers for her beautiful drawings. Nikki for putting it all together just the way I wanted.

Hilary and Jim, Mike and Liz for always helping me out and for being such good cooks. And Olive, Liz, Alex, Hannah, Rodrigo, Tom, and all the Dock Kitchen team.

Text © 2010 Stevie Parle
Illustrations © 2010 Ros Shiers
Design and layout © 2010
Quadrille Publishing Limited

To buy books in quantity for corporate use
or incentives, call **(800) 962–0973**
or e-mail **premiums@GlobePequot.com.**

First published in 2010 by
Quadrille Publishing Limited

First Lyons Press edition 2011

Lyons Press is an imprint of
Globe Pequot Press

Library of Congress Cataloging-in-Publication Data is available on file.

ISBN 978-0-7627-7034-2

Printed in China

10 9 8 7 6 5 4 3 2 1

Quadrille Publishing Limited
Alhambra House
27-31 Charing Cross Road
London WC2H 0LS
www.quadrille.co.uk

Editorial Director Anne Furniss
Creative Director Helen Lewis
Project Editor Lucy Bannell
Editor US edition Norma MacMillan
Designer Nicola Davidson
Illustrator Ros Shiers
Production Director Vincent Smith
Production Controller Ruth Deary

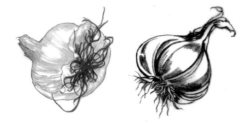